THE
REAL WITCHES'
GARDEN

THE

REAL WITCHES' GARDEN

KATE WEST

Element
An Imprint of HarperCollins*Publishers*
77–85 Fulham Palace Road,
Hammersmith, London W6 8JB

The website address is:
www.thorsonselement.com

and *Element* are trademarks of
HarperCollins*Publishers* Limited

Published by Element 2004

5 7 9 10 8 6 4

© Kate West, 2004

Kate West asserts the moral right to
be identified as the author of this work

Text illustrations by Chris Down

A catalogue record for this book
is available from the British Library

ISBN 0 00 716322 3

Printed and bound in Great Britain by
Scotprint, Haddington, East Lothian

CONTENTS

*This book is dedicated to
Mags who returned to the Goddess
in February 2003.
Her friendship and her presence in the
Craft are sorely missed.*

'May we meet and know love once again.'

ACKNOWLEDGEMENTS

Once again I am indebted to a great many people who made this book possible. So I would like to say a big thank you to the following:

My husband, partner and High Priest Steve, and our son Taliesin, for their patience, love and support.

The members of the now quite extensive family of the Hearth of Hecate for their continuing thoughts and positive energy. In particular to Mags for her wisdom on lunar gardening, Angela for her help with the children's section, Debs for being a sounding board, and Mike for his supportive friendship.

Merlyn and Epona of The Children of Artemis, for their hard work on behalf of the Craft, the Witches of today and those yet to come.

Andy Norfolk of AJN Landscape Consultants for his knowledge, practical help and advice.

All of our family and friends who have helped out in so many ways.

May the Old Gods watch over you all.

Blessed Be

FROM THE AUTHOR

Merry Meet!

If I were to ask you to describe a Witch's garden you would probably envisage climbers growing up the walls of a thatched cottage, a profuse array of colourful and traditional country-cottage-type plants, and herbs to tend all kinds of ailments. But the reality is often nowhere near the dream. For just as Witches appear just like everyone else, so their gardens are as varied as those of other people. They could be large or small; they may be a scrap of concrete, a window box or just the kitchen windowsill. They are often overlooked by neighbours, close to busy roads and shared with children and pets. We describe Witchcraft as a nature-based spirituality, but most of us do not live in an ideal rural idyll with a scenic cottage and enough land, let alone time, to have an established garden full of healing herbs and 'witchy' plants. We have busy lives with many commitments and little time to tend and love our herbs and plants. Whilst our Craft seeks to be one with the elements and the land, our personal 'land' may be a small scrap of ill-lit soggy soil, a wilderness of rocks and concrete, and full of discarded toys or the evidence of a love of dogs and cats! As Witches we seek to live as a part of the world, not apart from it, and hence we must be realistic. However, we can make the most of what we have, and tend it with a love of the land and of the Goddess, rather than wishing and waiting for some kind of ideal.

Firstly, let me say that this is not a gardening book in the usual way. Here I am not talking about 'how to garden'; making fertilizer, landscaping, installing water features, cement and decking, but rather how to make the most of your garden. How to use it as a part of your Craft, to make it a sacred place in its own right. A place where you can meet your Gods, where you can grow plants to help you work your magic. A place where you can pre-pay and repay the Goddess and the God, and the land, for what you take and are given. There will be ways of using your garden to enhance your Craft and ways of using your Craft to enhance your garden. Yes, there will be suggestions on what to plant, and how you might like to arrange them, but in the context of working from what you have, rather than creating a whole new outdoors!

Those of you who do have the luxury of being able to make a fresh start, in the fashion of so many modern gardening programmes, will be able to use the ideas here, but those of you with constraints on what you can do will still be able to take the ideas that do fit and discard the rest.

Whilst I have given some plant suggestions I am aware that, with a readership which includes the whole of the English-speaking world, you may not be able to grow the same things. So I have tried to give ideas of the types of plant rather than always being specific. It is my hope that, whatever your kind of soil type, climate, landscape, etc, you will be able to make use of this book. I also hope that you will try to do so using plants native to your area, as these are the ones with a magical connection to your land, your Goddesses and your Gods.

Let me also say that, in my life I have had the pleasure of keeping gardens of all shapes, sizes and conditions. These include a moderate-sized rural near-idyll, a walled but landscaped and shared green patch, many windowsills, 30 square feet of shaded concrete in an area of heavy industrial pollution, a landscaped, gravelled and decked modern travesty of the concept of contact with the earth, and just recently over 180 square metres of untended land given over to thistles! I've also worked in gardens where the concept of natural growth has been allowed to run riot, those with enough clay to start a decent-sized pottery, others where the half inch of topsoil covers several tons of concrete and rubble, and even one where the soil was made of, just for once, real growing-type earth! I've also shared my garden with dogs, cats, ardent sunbathers and various other life forms.

In this book I hope to incorporate ideas for all types of garden, or growing area, in ways which are compatible with having a full and busy life. Ways of being at one with the land, of sharing it with our near and dear, and still being able to work it in honour of the Goddess and the God. I will include lists of plants and herbs, not so that you can rush out and buy them all, but so that you can choose those which are most applicable to your life, your needs and your Craft.

And just as you can use your garden to celebrate and enhance your Craft, so too you can use magic to enhance your garden. Not everyone, not even those who practise the Craft, is blessed with 'green fingers', so here I shall also look at the magics you can work to enhance your 'green life': the seasons and times for the best results; spells for sowing, planting and growing, to protect delicate plants, to deter pests and even to influence the weather a little; the Goddesses and Gods who might look more favourably on your piece of the earth. This book is not intended to be the ultimate answer to all your gardening queries, but rather a starting point to blending what you have with what you would like.

As with all the other *Real Witches'* books this one is written for real people with real, busy lives who probably don't have huge amounts of time or money to spend on their gardens but who still want to become closer to the earth. Even if you have no interest in the Craft at all I hope that this book will be of interest to the gardener who seeks a more natural approach to what is, for some, our only work with nature.

Blessed Be

Kate

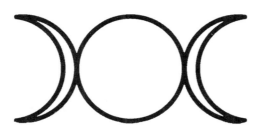

ONE

A NATURE-BASED BELIEF SYSTEM

I call on Earth to bind my spell,
Air to speed its passage well.
Bright as fire shall it glow,
And deep as ocean's tides shall flow.
Count the elements fourfold,
For in the Fifth the spell shall hold.
Blessed Be.

Why Witches and gardening? Witchcraft is often described as a nature-based spirituality but what does that mean? Well, early Witches would have worked and tended the land, cared for and healed the people and the livestock. Their daily lives and their magical work would have been for the prosperity and the future of their community. Indeed, it is in part from this that the traditional festivals, the Sabbats, came about. For in amongst the meanings of those festivals is a strong and continuing link to the Wheel of the Year and the seasons which form its basis. For me this was one of the key attractions of the Craft.

One of the ways of looking at the Sabbats is to refer them directly to the passage of the seasons. Very simply we can say that:

Samhain (31 October) marks the start of the resting season and is the harbinger of Winter whilst *Yule* (21 December) marks the onset of that season. *Imbolg* (2 February) brings the first buds and shoots rising through the frozen earth as a promise of the Spring which begins in earnest at *Oestara* (21 March). *Beltane* (1 May) when the hawthorn blossoms presages Summer and *Litha* (21 June) marks its beginning. *Lughnasadh* (1 August) is the first of the harvest, which reaches its height at *Madron* (21 September), the start of Autumn.

In the Craft we refer to the Sabbats collectively as the Wheel of the Year. In addition, each of these festivals is linked to the yearly cycles of the Goddess and the God. The Triple Goddess moves from Mother to Crone at Samhain, from Crone to Maiden at Imbolg, and from Maiden to Mother at Beltane. The God as her Consort moves alongside her through these changes as well as being the Oak and Holly Kings which preside over the lightening and darkening halves of the year from Yule to Litha and Litha to Yule, respectively.

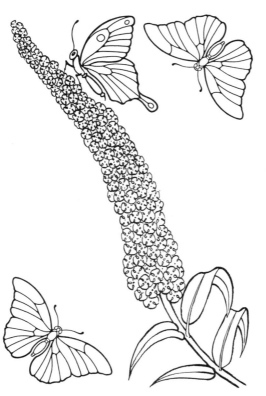

Not only do we celebrate the passage of the seasons but we draw our magical energy from them; Spring is a time of beginnings, Summer a time of development, Autumn the season of reaping and Winter is the time of rest. Of course from an agricultural perspective, that same seasonality tells us when to sow, tend, harvest and rest the soil. Whether from the perspective of the Witch or that of the gardener, the cycles which Witches celebrate as the Wheel of the Year and the phases of the Moon link everything together. There is a proper time for everything, and everything has its season.

The Magics that Witches work now,

as in the past, draw their energies directly from the elements of Air, Fire, Water and Earth, all of which are required to create growth and which, when imbued with the fifth element of Spirit, form the foundation of the Craft as well as our magic. Even the most non-natural magic, such as a working to keep your car on the road, derives its power from the energies of the elements. As the spell at the start of the chapter states, the elements are the key to working magic. Without true knowledge and under-standing of them it is not possible to work effective magic or to be an effective Witch. And there is no simpler or more natural way to gain that knowledge and understanding than by working with the elements in their most immediate form. For Witches, these are not just the external elements as seen in nature – wind, sun, rain and soil – but also the way those elements are part of ourselves and everything we do. Air is our thoughts, Fire our passions and enthusiasms, Water our emotions and Earth our physical selves. Spirit is the essential 'self' as well as the Goddess and the God both within and without. For us to understand and care for ourselves and each other, to develop and grow as individuals, and to work the magics which enhance the lives of our loved ones and our own community, we must harness and balance these elements, both within and without. This is a path of personal exploration, understanding and development which Witches use in all aspects of their daily lives, but perhaps nowhere more so than in their tending of life, whether it be in plants and the soil or in their relationships with family, friends and their wider community of the Craft.

The fifth element of Spirit is personified in the tales, legends and stories of the Goddess and the God, so many of whom are in turn linked to the fertility of the land, the crops, animals and people. From Amalthea, Goddess of plenty, to Zisa of the harvest, the Goddess is inextricably linked to fertility and growth. In her Lunar cycle of Maiden, Mother and Crone we think of her as planting, tending and reaping the life of the people, animals and the land. The God too holds these roles, the Horned God and the Corn King being probably the most obvious examples. There are Gods and Goddesses of sowing and planting, reaping and gathering, and of every kind of plant and animal, from belief systems of almost all times around the world (see Chapter 10 for some of these). Actually getting into contact with the elements and the soil brings special benefits in terms of direct contact with the Goddess and the God. Nowhere can you be closer to your Gods than when you are in touch with the life force that flows through the land than when you experience the elements in action, and when you can see the results of their magic which is the life of the land. And nowhere can you come to a greater understanding of the cycles of life, death and rebirth than when working with nature.

One of the other traditional key skills of the Witch is that of herbalist and healer. Witches have long been respected for their knowledge of healing plants and herbs, and many of these ancient remedies are being reintroduced into our daily lives now that the remedies of aromatherapy, homeopathy, etc, are becoming more readily available. Most practising Witches and other herbal therapists know, however, that these remedies are always better when they can be home-grown. And this is just another of the reasons why even the most urban of Witches feels the need to have some kind of practical connection with the earth.

There is another facet of the Craft which links practising Witches to the land and that is in the often forgotten relationship between the practise of magic and the payment for it. As the magic of Witches is worked in balance with the energies of the elements, as well as our personal energies, we must also look to returning something in kind. This is not just a question of repaying what we have been given, i.e. when the magic works, but should also take the form of pre-payment for what we might seek in the future. Whilst this can take the form of tending for the people in our lives and generally upholding the principles of the Craft, many Witches, myself among them, advocate actually working towards repaying nature itself. As I have mentioned in my other books, you could go to a local park or beauty spot and remove the debris and litter left by others, put food out for wild birds, or support an animal charity. But one of the most effective ways is to work the soil and to tend plants. Whilst you could do this in a local park or beauty spot, it is far more immediate and personally satisfying if you can do it in your own space, even if that space is restricted to a couple of pot plants on the windowsill.

But Witches do not just think of the tending of the garden in connection with the Craft. We use our gardens for the practice and enhancement of it. If we are fortunate and not too overlooked, we will be able to hold our Sabbat and Esbat (Full Moon) Rituals there. Casting the Circle outside, amongst the living reality of the Divine, adds a special dimension to our celebrations and workings. It enhances the magic. Even if we cannot practise obvious Rituals in the garden, we can still work our magic there; planting and growing spells, using the remedies that nature provides. We also use our gardens for contemplation, meditation and to grow closer to our Gods. And we find that, through being active and out there on the land we learn more about our Craft, and about healing not only the physical, but also the emotional and spiritual ills in our lives. Furthermore, being outside gives us the opportunity to get to know and understand more about the other living things we share our world with. Through observing the life around us, even if it's only a few sparrows and pigeons, we get to appreciate the natural cycles and rhythms in our own lives.

The aspects of the Craft covered in this book are those which relate directly to the care and use of the garden. For those of you for whom this is your first book on Witchcraft there is a fuller introduction and a selection of recommended reading in the appendices at the back of this book. Otherwise, let us move on to see how your garden can enhance your Craft and how the Craft can enhance your garden.

TWO

A SPACE FOR LIVING AND THE CRAFT

For many people the garden is the place where they go on the sunnier days of the year. It is a place for occasional barbecues, to have a drink with friends, perhaps to sunbathe or to banish the children when they get too noisy in the house. A few use it to grow herbs and perhaps vegetables for the kitchen. Many will use it to dry laundry, store bicycles and other outdoor equipment. For a Witch, the garden is all this and more. It is our piece of earth, our contact with nature, with the Goddess, the God and the Elements. It is where we grow healing herbs and plants to incorporate into our natural remedies and where we grow the sometimes quite toxic ingredients for inclusion in our incenses and magical spells. It is where we make payment for our magics and where we seek to do our part to enrich the cycle of life and living. It is where we honour the Goddess and the God in the most practical way we can, by tending their creation. It is where we work our Rituals to honour them and where we can work magics in their name, and also where we come to know and understand them through meditation and relaxation. It is where we can actually experience the cycles of the seasons and find the natural indicators for the Sabbats, where we can observe the phases of the Moon and where we can really get to know and understand the cycles of life, death and rebirth. In all of this it is also a place where we recharge our batteries, drawing energy from the earth itself and from our experience of the elements and their part in the rich pageant of growth. The Witches' garden can also be where we seek to preserve endangered plants and provide a refuge for wildlife. To a Witch, the garden is more than an outdoor room, it is a permanent Sacred Space in its own right, even when being used to hang the washing or amuse the young.

The first thing you need to do is to work out what you really have, what you want and need from it, and what you actually can do. Yes, I currently have a reasonable-sized garden but this is a rented property and so, because it is not truly mine, there are limitations on what I can and cannot do to it. I cannot cut down any trees, move the drive, nor replace the gravelled surface with the thyme and chamomile lawn I would so dearly love to have. Furthermore, I have a young son, so anything I do has to

respect his need for a play area, or accept the devastation that a quick game of football might do to my carefully hatched plans! You also almost certainly have constraints on what you can do. These may be like mine, imposed from outside, or they might be the views of other family members, those of nature herself or personal ones like the amount of time and effort you can afford to expend. However, whatever the limitations there is always some kind of way around them. So let us look at some of these issues and some of the potential solutions.

WHAT DO YOU REALLY WANT TO USE IT FOR?

In the following chapters I shall look more closely at some of the ways of actually using your garden as a Sacred Space, a space for working magic and celebrating the Sabbats;

a place of contemplation and meditation, to grow herbs and other useful plants; a place dedicated to your favourite or personal deities; even a place where you can introduce your children to a love of nature. But you also need to take into account the non-Craft activities you enjoy. If you like sunbathing, then you will need an unshaded space to stretch out in. If you want to hold summer barbecues, then a place where you will not set fire to, or scorch, your plants is essential. If, like me, the winter wind howls across the landscape, then you will need to retain a windbreak hedge. To help you to plan the potential uses of your garden, write a month by month list of the sorts of things you want to do outside, the difficulties they pose and your ideas for solutions. You may find you come up with some difficulties to which you cannot think of an answer. Don't despair, keep your list for a few months while you look around, watch TV gardening programmes and read books; it can be surprising how much inspiration the Goddess will provide to the patient.

HOW MUCH SPACE DO YOU HAVE?

If you have a reasonable-sized garden, that is well and good, but for those of you with little or no outdoors of your own, try to consider the following: Do you have room to securely fix one or more window boxes? Can you use indoor windowsills? Can you place a table or perhaps a bookcase in front of a window and use that space? If you have a light room, could you perhaps denote a corner or patch to be an indoor garden area? Perhaps you could even transform a gloomy corner. When it comes to the garden as a part of your Craft you do not need much – a reasonable-sized tub on a waterproof dish, or a couple of pots on your windowsill can easily be enough. Chapter 9 focuses on the non-existent, or almost non-existent, garden.

WHAT IS IT CURRENTLY BEING USED FOR?

One of the problems of a garden is that it quickly becomes a multifunctional area, often to the detriment of its garden aspect. Parked cars, secured bikes, children's toys, washing lines, dustbins and so on all take from your natural space. Not that these things aren't compatible with growing things and celebrating the Craft, but you may need to give some thought to maximizing your usable space. This could be as simple, if not always easy, as encouraging others to put their things away. On the other hand you might like to think about finding ways of storing things more sympathetically; hooks in a garage, or a storage 'bin' into which odds and ends can be packed. One of my somewhat unusual solutions lies in having a large second-hand filing cabinet in the garage. This stores, in a vertical rather than horizontal space, a wide miscellany of outdoor toys, gardening bits and things we have no use for, but are reluctant to get rid of yet! Some of the things you keep outside of the home cannot be put away, dustbins and coalbunkers for example, but they needn't look quite so ugly. Consider planting climbers on, or in pots around, such items.

WHO ELSE USES IT?

Most of us have to share our garden in some way or another; perhaps with family members who may not practise the Craft, with children who want a play area or with pets who see it as an area of convenience! Not only that, but few of us have the luxury of complete privacy, as so many of today's gardens are overlooked, or what takes place in them can be overheard. Whilst you can always attempt to place plants in such a way as to minimize this, you don't want to end up with no natural light ever reaching your garden, or for that matter the windows of your home! Also give some thought to the safety aspect.

For example, ponds and toddlers, yours or visiting, don't mix. But if you carefully fill your pond with large stones, you can still grow your water plants and keep the young ones safe. Steps, concrete or stone corners and other sharp edges are likewise a hazard to the very young, the very old and the infirm. If these features are already present, consider putting up guard rails, or other obvious identifiers. If you need them as part of your plan, think about rounded edges, or using wood instead.

HOW WILL YOUR ENVIRONMENT AND CLIMATE AFFECT YOUR PLANS?

Soil type, weather, rainfall, drainage, pollution and so on should also be taken into account. The problems they pose are not insoluble, but give them some thought or you could end up expending a lot of energy counteracting a series of inherent conditions.

The type of soil you have will influence the kinds of plants which will grow in it. Of course you could strip off your topsoil and have it replaced, but that is somewhat extreme and not cheap! Dig a small hole about 8 inches deep and have a good look at what you've got. Too much clay and it will be heavy, hard to drain and may set like concrete in the Summer. Too much sand and it will drain freely and dry out quickly in hot weather. Both of these problems can be helped by digging in some organic matter. A friend of mine recently had several tons of 'mature' pig manure delivered free, by a farmer only too glad to get rid of it, but this is a bit extreme. Create your own quick compost by sweeping up Autumn leaves and storing them in bin liners until they get smelly. Dig this through and it will help no end. It is also a good idea to test the pH balance of the soil; you can get kits from your garden centre. If your soil is particularly acid or alkaline (chalky), try to choose plants which like these conditions, and grow others either in pots or in 'wells' which you have lined generously with potting compost.

Give some thought to local rainfall and the water table. If your 8-inch hole rapidly filled up with water, you're probably in a damp zone! If in doubt, your local radio weather forecaster may be able to answer a patient enquiry, and you could ask them about hours of sunshine and average temperatures at the same time; alternatively, have a look on the Internet. Too little water is relatively easy to fix, as you can collect rainwater in a barrel and water regularly, but a damp climate will never suit plants which prefer to grow in the desert!

Spend a day tracking the amount of direct light falling onto your garden (it's easier to do when the Sun is shining). This will tell you where best to plant sun-, or shade-, loving plants.

Take a look at the kinds of industry in your area, for about 5 miles around! If there's anything that seems likely to produce pollution, seek out tolerant plants. Take a look at roadside growing areas around you, with a good field guide handy, for some really good clues. Also, talk to your neighbours or take a quick look over their fences, briefly to avoid embarrassment, and see what's doing well there, to give you some ideas.

HOW WILL YOU AFFECT LOCAL WILDLIFE?

Please give a thought to local flora and fauna. Check out holes and tracks to see whether they are in use. A light dusting of cornflour will easily show up prints. Be considerate with weedkillers, insecticides, fertilizers, hedge trimmers and when digging up stuff. If you have huge amounts of weeds, or a thicket of brambles, they're probably doing a good job of feeding birds, growing caterpillars and so on. Don't remove these sanctuaries all in one go, plant a refuge in an inconspicuous corner, or clear a portion at a time. Rampant growth is usually good for creatures which benefit the garden, so if you banish them you may acquire all kinds of interesting problems which you could have avoided. Try to find a corner for nettles, brambles and a small heap of decaying wood, as this will attract beneficial insects.

To take your Craft into your garden, whatever it's like, it is first important to assess what you have got and what you need from it. Being a Witch is being a part of reality so you have to take into account the physical constraints of your location, family and life, not to mention the amount of time and effort you can really devote to it. Having said that, with a little ingenuity, you can make a big difference with just a little thought and effort.

One of the ways of assessing your patch of earth is to look at those around you – if your neighbourhood is knee-deep in lavender then there's a good chance it will grow in your garden too! Established plants in your garden and those of your neighbours will give you a good indication of soil and climate type.

If you move into a new house, and if you can possibly bear to, wait one year to see what is already in the garden. Or maybe you could ask the previous occupiers if they have any photos, as proud gardeners often do.

The following chapters contain ideas for different ways of designing and using your garden to enhance your Craft. It is not intended that you use all of these ideas, indeed you would need a vast area to do so! Rather take those which most appeal to you and will fit your garden and your life style. Feel free to adapt them, or to use them as a starting point from which to create something personal.

THREE

THE GARDEN AS YOUR SACRED SPACE

As I have often said, Witches do not have special buildings or even rooms set aside as places of Ritual and Magic. We create our Sacred Space wherever and whenever we need it. To do this we need a clear area, large enough for the number of people who are to take part. We then invoke the elements of Air, Fire, Water and Earth and invite the Goddess and the God. When working magic, rather than simply celebrating the festivals, we also cast a Circle, which contains the energies raised until it is time to release them. At the end of our working, we then remove the Circle, banish the elements and thank the Goddess and God. It is also usual to have some kind of Altar within the Circle, onto which we place representations of the elements, the Goddess and the God, and any working tools and equipment we may need during our working. This is also cleared away at the end. However, as the Craft is a nature-based belief system, it is always nice to be able to practise at least some of it, weather permitting, outside alongside nature and the elements.

Practising the Craft outside has certain differences; obviously you do not need to take representations of the elements outside, they are there in the air, sun- and moonlight, rain and soil. The Goddess and the God are also present as they are the life force which causes everything to grow, and are seen in the cycles of life, death and rebirth which are all around. If you intend to use your garden, or a part of it, as a Sacred Space, you can therefore install and care for its components as a part of your usual gardening life. There are many levels of doing this from a complete garden makeover to the more practical placement of one or two plants and objects which are less obtrusive. Here I shall look at a few ideas for a complete makeover, but will focus more on the simpler approach.

PLANNING YOUR SACRED SPACE

In an ideal world you could have a lawn shaped as the triple moon, or as a circle with the pentagram picked out in flat stones or bricks. I even know of one garden where the owner has created a pentacle with small paving stones and has planted different plants and herbs in each of the different sections. You could also perhaps place elemental markers at the appropriate points, either plants or actual physical representations such as wind chimes in the east for Air, an outdoor flame or torch for Fire, a pond or fountain for Water in the west and a large stone in the north for Earth. This stone could also double as your Altar, or you could have a second Altar stone in the centre. If the area is not overhung with trees, or otherwise likely to suffer from fire damage, you could dig a permanent fire pit in the centre, or even have a permanent cauldron. If you wish, and can find reasonable ones, you could also place a statue of the Goddess and the God in the north of your Circle. Traditionally, the Witches' circle is 9 feet (2.75 m) across, but if you will be working on your own it can be smaller. Around your circle you could place plants which act as screens for privacy, as well as those which are related to the elements, the Goddesses and Gods of your choice, or even those which are associated with the Wheel of the Year. Chapter 10 gives lists of plant associations.

However, most of us do not have the luxury of being able to not only start from scratch but also of being able to let our Craft dominate the use of even a part of the garden. In this case you may like to take ideas from the above and incorporate them into your existing space or use some of the following suggestions.

Firstly, you need to determine where the four quarters lie. This can be achieved precisely by using a compass, or more simply by noting where the Sun rises (in the east) and sets (west) and working from there. You do not have to be precise. In each of the quarters place a single plant in the colour of that element; yellow in the east, red in the south, blue in the west and green in the north. Of course they may well not be in flower all year round but nevertheless they will be present as reminders. If you really do not have the room to make these permanent fixtures, keep your plants in pots and put them in place only when needed. Alternatively, you could have a plant which rustles in the east, a sundial in the south, a birdbath in the west and a special stone or rock in the north.

Try to incorporate a permanent Altar, although it need not be too obvious. Whilst you do not need a large area onto which you can put a great many things, at the very least it is a good idea to have somewhere safe to place a candle, usually in a jar to protect it from the wind. This could be a small flat stone or rock. The Altar can be placed in a number of parts of the Circle, for example, the east as the point of beginning, or the centre, or the north, which is known as the place of power. Generally speaking, a rock in the centre of your area is likely to be an inconvenience, as it may well get in the way of any outdoor activities. If it is in the centre of a lawn it will cause complications when mowing, and it will almost certainly give rise to comments from friends and neighbours. So this leaves you with the choice of north or east. If you really can't leave something permanently then try to choose something you can easily and safely move from one place to another. A small outdoor table or even a stool can make a good substitute for a rock or stone, and is much easier to move around!

Privacy is a much harder problem to overcome. If you start erecting screens in your garden, you are more likely to increase the interest of your neighbours than decrease it. If you try to grow plants which will effectively obstruct their view of you, these may well give rise to complaints about the amount of light their garden receives, not to mention cast your area into the shade. And whilst it would be nice to think that it's none of their business what you get up to in your garden, you will still have to live alongside these people. A little eccentricity may well be tolerated, but a full-blown Witches' gathering is almost certainly going to be too much! In reality, the only solution is to temper what you do and how you do it. So, if you are overlooked, you may have to give up ideas of working skyclad or even robed, and you may also have to consider whether Circle dancing, chanting and drumming are going to be acceptable. Of course, if you work on your own you probably don't do all these things anyway, as solitary Craft does not require you to wave your arms or speak aloud, but do give some thought as to how you may appear to someone looking out of their window on a moonlit night. For the Witch on their own, simple screening, such as encouraging a climber or two in the direct line of sight, is often enough to give you the peace you need.

Once you have determined where and how to mark your Sacred Space you need to bless, dedicate and consecrate it. This is done in several steps. Firstly, before you start any work on the area, ask the blessing of the Goddess and the God. Secondly, as you work, dedicate your efforts to the Goddess and the God. Thirdly, perform a Ritual to consecrate the space. The best time of year to do this would be Spring, when nature is ready to put fresh effort into growth. But there is no reason why you should not commence at other seasons and continue the work thereafter. Chapter 8 gives advice on the seasonality of sowing, planting and reaping.

SEEKING THE BLESSING OF THE GODDESS AND THE GOD

Work for this should commence prior to the New Moon as you will need to collect about a pint of rainwater. If your area is very arid then try to collect water from a stream or river and bring it back to your garden. If this really is not possible then you will need to take tap water and place it in a sealed jar in the light of the Full Moon for three nights and then wait for the next New Moon to continue. You will also need to make an asperger. This is done by taking a few thin twigs about 6 to 8 inches (15 to 20 cm) in length and tying them at one end to make a sort of 'mini-broom'. If you can, gather these twigs from fallen wood found in your own garden, otherwise collect them from a nearby wooded area.

At the New Moon, the time of fresh starts and new beginnings, take your water, asperger and some salt outside into the garden. In the centre of your future Sacred Space, kneel and call, using visualization, each of the elements coming from their appropriate directions. Next, visualize the Goddess and the God and invite them to be with you. When you are sure all is in place, take a pinch of salt and add it to the water, saying, in your head:

'I call upon the elements and upon the Old Gods to consecrate and bless this water. May it drive out all impurities and may it bring the love of the Goddess and the God to this place. Blessed Be.'

Now with your asperger, sprinkle a little of the water around the outside edge of your Circle. Be sure to start at the north-east and to proceed deosil (clockwise) around the Circle until you have overlapped at the north-east. Return to the centre, once again visualize the Goddess and the God, and say:

'I call upon the Goddess and the God of life and all things living, to grant that this may be a place of growth, for all the life that shall use it. May it ever be a place of joy, love and magic. May it aid me to honour the Gods and the Craft. Blessed Be.'

Remain a while and visualize the area as you hope it to be, and visualize yourself using it. When you are ready, thank the elements and the Goddess and the God. Where there is more than one of you taking part, everyone should perform the same actions, one after the other.

DEDICATING YOUR SACRED SPACE

This is not a Ritual but rather an ongoing process which takes place whilst you do the work on your Sacred Space.

Over the next two weeks, and indeed any time you need to tend your area, always start by visualizing the Goddess and the God. Ask their blessing and state that you are dedicating this work to them. An effective way of doing this is to gather any gardening tools together into the centre of your space and then to close your eyes for a moment.

Visualize the Goddess and the God and say:

'I call upon the Old Gods to witness this work which I do in their honour. May they guide and support me in this as in all things. Blessed Be.'

Then continue your work. If you are simply making a few changes or additions to your existing garden then do not forget to tend other plants; dead-heading flowers past their best, removing dead wood or weeding between existing plants. For most people, the two weeks between the New and Full Moons will be sufficient for them to carry out the work in the garden. But if your plans are more complex, you are planting many new plants or your workload is heavier, then you may need to continue to work through the next lunar period, before consecrating your Sacred Space at a subsequent Full Moon. It is more important to be thorough than to hurry, as you are creating a permanent Sacred Space, and besides, nature, like the Goddess, takes her own time.

CONSECRATING YOUR SACRED SPACE

The ritual of Consecration could take place at the next Full Moon, but it is important that any plants have had time to establish themselves as it can be very disheartening to find that perhaps one or two specimens were not as good as you hoped and wither or die just after your Ritual! So if you are not sure they have had time to settle in it might be better to wait until the following Full Moon.

Once all is in place and you are happy that any plants are established, it is time to hold your Ritual. You will need: A small glass containing some wine or fruit juice.

Start at the east and say, either quietly or in your head:

'I call upon the element of Air. Mighty winds and gentle breezes be present here, each in its turn and in its season. Watch over this space, those that live, work and play in it, and all that takes place in it. May the Air of thought and inspiration be ever strong here. Blessed Be.'

Move to the south and say:

'I call upon the element of Fire. May the Sun which warms and lights all life be present here, in due course and due season. Watch over this space; those that live, work and play in it, and all that takes place in it. May the Fire of passion and enthusiasm be ever strong here. Blessed Be.'

Move to the west and say:

'I call upon the element of Water. Great storms and gentle rains be present here, each in its turn and in its season. Watch over this space; those that live, work and play in it, and all that takes place in it. May the Water of joy and emotion be ever strong here. Blessed Be.'

Move to the north and say:

'I call upon the element of Earth. Strong rocks and life-giving soil, be present here, in the land and in ourselves. Watch over this space; those that live, work and play in it, and all that takes place in it. May the Earth of our bodies be ever strong here. Blessed Be.'

Remain at the north point, visualize the Goddess and the God, and say:

'I call upon the Mother Goddess, giver of life, death and rebirth. I call upon God the Hunter and Hunted, spirit of the Land. Be with this place, with all that grows here and with all who pass through it. Guide us, guard us and protect us in this and all we do. This place is Sacred to you and a marker of love to you. Blessed Be.'

Now take the glass of wine (or fruit juice), hold it up to the Goddess and the God and say:

'This wine is my offering to the Goddess and the God. As it pours onto the earth may their love flow also into the land.'

Walk around your circle and sprinkle a little wine as you go. Try to ensure that you scatter it evenly and that you have a little left at the end. When you have completed the Circle hold the glass up once more and say:

'As the Goddess and God sustain the land, may they likewise sustain those who work with it. Blessed Be.'

Take a small drink yourself. If you are performing this with others then you should refill the glass after going around the Circle and then pass the glass around everyone present so that they may have a sip after the 'Blessed Be'.

Next, take a few moments to meditate and reflect on your Sacred Space and on the things you will be doing in it. Lastly, return to each of the quarters and thank the elements, but do not dismiss them, and finally thank the Goddess and the God.

Your Sacred Space is now ready for any future use. As with indoor Rituals you will still need to invoke and banish the elements, and to invite and thank the Goddess and the God, each time you use it. But their residual energies will always be present, and should enhance not only the feeling of the working space but also the health of the plants which are growing there.

CONTINUING CARE OF YOUR SACRED SPACE

It goes without saying that you cannot expect a garden, or portion thereof, to remain static. Nature is boundless, resourceful and energetic, and plants will continue to grow, whether you've planned it that way or not! It is therefore a good idea to set aside a little time to tend your Sacred Space on a regular basis. Many Witches I know like to do this just before the Full Moon and the Sabbats. Not only is this just before they intend to use it and hence leaves it in the best possible condition for their Rituals, but they are also, for the practising Witch, easy times to remember.

I find that one of the most difficult aspects in tending the outdoor Sacred Space lies not so much in finding the time to plant and grow, but in finding the strength of mind to uproot and cut back. It can easily seem somehow ungrateful to take away the excess growth! However, you do have to be fairly firm, as a garden allowed to run riot will quickly turn into a wild place where some species, like mint, can take over to the detriment of slower-growing, less prolific species. Many plants have special requirements and there is certainly no room in a book like this to list them all, but as a general rule of thumb, Spring and Autumn are the best seasons for major pruning and trimming. Many gardeners recommend doing your major trimming in the Spring, as this gives the plant the benefit of improving weather to re-establish itself. However, it is worth mentioning that a good prune in the Autumn after the plant has flowered and seeded, can give it a good chance to show its best in Summer and to rest over the Winter, as well as the ability to produce a healthy new generation of seedlings for

the following year. Privet is a good example of this as a Spring prune often results in no flowers, whereas an Autumn one allows the plant to flower. Furthermore, Autumn pruning is less likely to disturb nesting birds.

Whenever you tend your Sacred Space, follow the same approach as you did above for dedicating it. Indeed, any part of working on your garden or home will benefit from the same approach, as dedicating your work to the Goddess and the God has the effect of making the task easier to complete and more effective.

USING YOUR OUTDOOR SACRED SPACE

The drawbacks of an outdoor working space are easy to understand. Unless you are very fortunate in your climate, the weather is likely to play a major part in determining whether it is reasonable to work outside. This is not only because it is hard to maintain focus in the pouring rain or strong wind, but also because you will be that much more conspicuous to any observers if you spend time outside in inclement conditions. The advantages, though, are well worth the effort of developing and maintaining one. Having your own outdoor space means that when you feel the need to be closer to nature you do not have to seek out a working area on public land, with all its attendant complications, such as dog walkers, stray policemen, etc. Nor do you have to carry any tools or equipment for miles. Your space is there for you, whenever you need it, and conveniently close to hand.

As has been mentioned elsewhere in this book, Witches tend to work their magic at the Full Moons and celebrate the festivals or Sabbats. Some will also work at other lunar phases, especially the New Moon. An outdoor Sacred Space is particularly good for celebrating the Sabbats, as these are closely linked to the passage of the seasons. It is always going to be far easier to feel in tune with the seasons when you can see, hear, feel, smell and even taste them all around you. At Imbolg, for example, you are not just thinking of the buds on the trees, you can see them. For this reason a good many Witches who use an outdoor space will celebrate the major Sabbats at the times of the seasonal markers, rather than on the calendar dates they have subsequently been given. So Imbolg would be held when the first buds or lambs are seen, Beltane when the hawthorn (or may) blossoms, Lughnasadh when the first of the harvest is coming in and Samhain when the first storms of Winter arrive.

Many people still have the image of Witches working at the dead of night. This has been so in the past for fear of discovery and today is often so with a group or Coven as it is the time when daily life is complete and everyone is free. But Witches on their own do not need to wait for darkness to fall, they can work whenever suits them. With an outdoor space you can perform your magic at any time of day.

An outdoor Sacred Space is particularly good for working magic relating to the cycles of nature; for spells affecting fertility, plants, animals and healing. All these benefit from, and are stronger for being worked close to the land. As mentioned above, when working outside you do not need to summon the elements in the same way as you would for an indoor Ritual. Nor will you need representations of them on your Altar, as they are all around. It is enough to turn to face each quarter and call upon the elements in turn, making sure that you recall each one's personal associations as well as the external ones. You then invite the Goddess and the God as usual. Of course it is still important to remember at the end of your Ritual to thank all the elements and deities which you have called.

An outdoor Sacred Space is also useful for other magical steps which may not be a part of a spell or Ritual. When you need to place something in the light of the Full Moon, then the centre of your space is an excellent place to put it, so long as you remember to remove it before any children or pets can interfere. The centre is also a good spot to place any poorly plants which you intend to nurse back to health. Of course this latter, like many Craft activities, should be tempered with common sense. There is no use putting a sensitive tropical houseplant out into the Winter's snow and expecting it to thrive!

A HEALING SPELL FOR PLANTS

There are very few Witches or gardeners around who do not, sooner or later, have a poorly plant or two. It is important firstly to ensure that any obvious causes have been addressed: if you have been away for two weeks and the poor thing received no water, then water it; if it is infested with some kind of parasite then remove the offending bugs and so on. But once these practical steps have been addressed then it is time to use magic to help it on its way back to health.

At some point during the Waxing Moon take your plant to your Sacred Space, place it either in the centre or upon your Altar. You will also need a small amount of rainwater in a shallow dish or bowl.

Call upon the quarters, starting with the east; saying:

'I call thee O element of Air, to give your healing strength to this (name the plant) … Blessed Be.'

Then move to the south, west and north calling upon Fire, Water and Earth, respectively. Now stand facing the north and invite the Goddess and the God, saying:

'I call upon the Goddess, Mother of all living, and the God, Lord of the Land to aid me in healing this (name of plant) … Lend your strength to it and watch over it, that it might flourish in your name.'

Wait until you can clearly visualize their presence, then say:

'Blessed Be.'

You can either use the names of the Goddess and God which you most favour working with, or you could use those with particular associations for the plant in question.

Now take the water and draw an invoking Pentagram [see chapter 5, page 43, for description] **in it with your finger or Athame** [see Terms and Definitions], **then hold it up to the Goddess and the God and say:**

'May this water be blessed and consecrated by the Gods. May it purify and heal this plant. Blessed Be.'

With your fingertips sprinkle a little of the water over the plant's foliage and then pour the remainder into the soil around it. Thank the elements by going back to each quarter, starting with the east as before, and saying:

'I give thanks to thee O element of Air. May your strength ever watch over this place. Blessed Be.'

Repeat for the south, west and north. Then, facing the north, visualize the Goddess and the God and say:

'I give thanks to the Goddess and the God for aiding me. May their light ever shine here and on all that dwells in this place. Blessed Be.'

Assuming that the weather is clement, or reasonably so, leave the plant there for three days and nights before returning it to a suitable location.

If the plant is not in a pot then you will need to take a small cutting or sprig into the Circle with you, so that it is represented there. Consecrate and bless the water as above but keep it on the Altar until your Ritual is completed. Then take the water out of the Circle to the plant and sprinkle and water as above.

Of course, not everyone's celebration of the Craft takes the form of active Circle work, but there are other ways we can bring nature into our magic and magic into nature.

FOUR

THE GARDEN FOR THE GODDESS AND THE GOD

In the Craft we believe that there are many facets of the Divine. Individual Goddess and God forms have different attributes and characteristics, such as Aphrodite Goddess of Love, Mercury God of Communication, Herne Lord of the Forest,

Cerridwyn Goddess of Wisdom, and many, many more. All of them, however, are linked to the cycles of life, death and rebirth, and all are in some way linked to nature and the land. Thus it is through nature, the plants, trees and herbs, etc, that we can become closer to them; closer to understanding their nature and more able to connect with them. Just as there are many Goddesses and Gods there are many ways of celebrating them within your garden – even a single plant can be your offering to the Divine. Chapter 10 lists some plants which are linked to different aspects of the Goddess and the God. But you can also dedicate a corner, or even the whole space, to a design which will help you to develop a closer relationship.

The first step is to decide which aspects of the Divine you intend to honour in the space you have available to you. If you have been practising the Craft for a while, you will already be aware of the Goddess and God forms to which you feel closest. You may even have some idea of how you would like to do this. However, you may prefer to honour the Divine in a less specific way, simply having an area set aside for meditation and contemplation of them in general. There are many shapes which are linked to the Divine and which can be introduced into your plans, such as the spiral, the triple moon ☽○☾ , tall phallic shapes for the God of fertility, and even animal shapes such as the deer, hare, cat, etc.

This part of your garden then becomes a place where not only can you contemplate your Gods, but also a place where you can get away from the hustle and bustle of daily life; a place where you can go to meditate, or just to relax and unwind.

PLANNING THE AREA

In my garden I have plans to introduce a spiral walkway of flat stones into one of the beds. The spiral is an ancient symbol of the Goddess, and can be found carved into many monoliths, cave walls and even pieces of jewellery. It is felt that the spiral represents the path both inwards and outwards to enlightenment and truth. Today, you will often find spiral paths created at Pagan and Wiccan events so that we too can follow this ancient tradition. My garden walkway will serve the dual purpose of giving me easier access to the plants in this space as well as providing a contemplative walk. Designing and crafting a spiral on the ground is not easy, but perhaps the best method is to map it out on squared paper and then to place a grid (use string tied to sticks placed in the ground) over the area you intend to use, so that you can repeat your design. It is common to find at the centre of the spiral a destination, perhaps a fountain, a sundial or a flat rock for sitting on. Alternatively, you can place your most meaningful, or loved, plant at this point. Of course it is not necessary to have a spiral large enough to walk on, you could just as easily use pebbles in a small container which you can trace with your finger or eye. Around this you might like to plant one of the smaller scented herbs such as a miniature thyme or even some alpines. It is worth mentioning that, contrary to the beliefs of some, the spiral is not just a symbol of the Goddess as Crone, although that is sometimes its primary attribution. It also symbolizes the Triple Goddess and some aspects of the God in terms of the cycles of life, death and rebirth.

I also know of someone who hopes to convert their whole lawn into a triple moon, but it is not necessary for this shape to take over your whole garden. The 〴〡〵 can be incorporated into flower beds, or with a little ingenuity you could divide it into its three sections and, by placing one in each of three pots, have a triple moon which can be lined up. When it comes to defining shapes in the ground you can use stones or pebbles, wood shavings (although do make sure they come from a good source) or even other plants to define the edges. If you are using plants to create shapes try to select ones which do not grow rampantly; mint, for example, can take over a whole garden if left to its own devices! A better choice would be some of the low level annuals and/or bedding plants; lobelia is one which I find relatively easy to train and control.

These days it is relatively easy to introduce animal shapes into the garden as many garden centres sell pre-formed woven wicker shapes which are intended for use in training climbing plants such as ivy, jasmine, honeysuckle, clematis and so on. These come in a variety of sizes, from those intended to support shrubs and bushes to ones small enough to be placed in a pot with the plant of your choice. Alternatively, if you are artistic, you can draw these shapes in the ground and then 'colour in' with the plants of your choice.

Some Witches prefer the idea of creating a number of small 'shrines' to different Goddesses and Gods. These can be fairly elaborate with statues and areas to place candles and offerings, or they can be simpler. One idea is to select a plant specific to each Goddess or God you wish to honour in this way, and to place before each of these plants a fairly small marker stone, which can be used to place a nightlight on at the times when you wish to interact with or commune with that deity.

An alternative idea is to simply create a quiet corner, where it is possible to sit in peace and to meditate. If you can, try to place this in such a way that the intended view is of plants and trees, rather than the house or road, which can easily distract your thoughts. You may find that you have to plant something in your direct line of sight to achieve this. Near to where I live there is a wild flower and wildlife centre which has a chamomile seat which would be ideal for this purpose. They have created a raised 'box'

from logs and placed willow 'arms' and a 'back' to form a chair. The seat is sown with chamomile and the willow has been allowed to root into the ground. The willow is kept regularly trimmed and woven back into shape, so that the seat can actually be sat upon. I feel, however, that this is probably an idea for the gardener who has plenty of time to devote to tending just one part of the garden. Having said that, there is no reason why you should not create an archway around an existing piece of furniture, or around a space where you can place your chair, or cushion. Pre-formed bamboo arches are ideal for this purpose, and can be used to support climbing plants. You can even do this indoors, linking two pots with the arch and training the plants to meet in the middle, so long as you are sure that you will be able to leave the plants in position.

It is worth mentioning here that, when dealing with climbers, you do need to be patient. It is tempting to encourage them upwards as fast as you can, but you will get a better effect by training them backwards and forwards in horizontal zig-zags, so that the foliage is fairly dense all the way up. Otherwise you can end up surrounded by the stems, with the leaves and flowers all being over your head!

Of course, a quiet corner does not have to take the form of a seat or bower. Another of my projects is to create a crescent-moon-shaped bed, raised perhaps 6 to 9 inches (15 to 25 cm) above the surrounding soil, so that I can create an area of tranquillity within it. I plan to plant the upper surface of the bed with some of the taller, traditional 'cottage garden' plants such as hollyhock, delphiniums, foxgloves, etc. This will not entirely preclude the surrounding sights and sounds but will mean that when seated on the ground, I am in the midst of the plants. As I also hope to attract butterflies, bees and other wildlife I shall also include plants such as buddleia and, against the nearby fence, wisteria. To enhance the relaxation element of the area, and because it is significant to my region, I shall include lavender. As this is to be an area with little 'traffic' I intend to plant a thyme or chamomile 'lawn' in the centre of the crescent. In the past, when my space has been limited, I have kept some plants in pots which can be arranged around me when I need a place of quiet, and again you can utilize this idea within the home.

Obviously, when choosing the site of your quiet area, you will need to take into account the layout of your garden, and the place most likely to be relatively quiet, but it is always useful to seek the guidance and blessing of the Gods.

SEEKING THE BLESSING OF THE GODDESS AND THE GOD

Before you seek the guidance and blessing of the Gods make, buy or seek out an offering for them. This could be a circle of plaited grasses, a single flower head, or perhaps a significantly shaped stone you have found on a walk. It could be a plant you have raised especially for the purpose. It need not be expensive, but should be something which has required you to make a special effort. Offerings to the Old Ones should always entail a sacrifice of time or effort. Of course, your major offering in any garden-related project will be the ongoing time and effort you place into creating and maintaining that area, but this will be a token of that effort.

At a time when you will be undisturbed, take your token out into your garden, close your eyes and visualize the Goddess and the God. Call upon them and ask them to guide you to a place of peace and tranquillity saying:

'I call upon the Goddess and the God. Lord and Lady I seek a place in which to know you, a place in which to understand you. Show me the way, that I might draw closer to you in peace and love. Give me an open heart and a fresh mind that I might see your way. Blessed Be.'

Holding their image in your mind, turn slowly around three times and open your eyes. Look over the whole of your garden with these thoughts in your head and you will surely be able to see the best location for your new space. If you are considering placing your area indoors use the same invocation to help you to determine the best place. Once you have found the right spot, walk to it, close your eyes again and say:

'I give thanks to the Goddess and the God for showing me the way. I undertake to work and tend this place in their name in gratitude for their love, and in token of this I make this offering. Blessed Be.'

Place your token in the centre of the area. If you have a particular deity or deities in mind then you can call upon these by name and choose your offering specifically with them in mind.

I find it useful to mark off any area I am about to work on with a few canes tied together with string. This has the effect of alerting my young son and his friends that this is not a play area, thus allowing me a clear working space and giving any plants time to establish themselves. It also encourages me to get on with the job, as sticks and string make it obvious that work has not been completed!

Having located your quiet area you need to work on it and to Dedicate it.

DEDICATING THE AREA

As with the preceding chapter, dedication is more of a process than an event. Remember to visualize the Goddess and the God every time you work on the area, and ask them to help you. Apart from the aspect of making the place special to them, any task dedicated to the Gods benefits from their energies and will therefore be easier and more successful. Try to leave one small, last task in the preparation of your area for your rite of dedication. Perhaps a last prune or trim, or maybe the placing of a single plant or object.

CONSECRATING THE AREA

Once you have set up your area to your satisfaction then you will want to consecrate it. It is best to do this at the Full Moon and at the time of day when you feel you are most likely to be using the site for meditation, contemplation or just to be closer to nature and the Gods. For some this will be early evening, but it could just as easily be any other time of the day. For me this is in the morning, after the 'school run' but before I actually start working, as I find that a few moments with the Gods both clears the mind and helps to inspire me.

Take with you into the area some water in a suitable watering vessel, a chalice with a little wine, or fruit juice, and any tools you may need for that last small task which you saved. Place all these to one side of your area, settle yourself down and compose yourself. If it is safe to do so, remove your shoes and go barefoot, so that you are in actual contact with the earth. Spend a few minutes in silent contemplation of both the area and the Goddess and the God. I find it helps to focus on my breathing for a couple of moments before I start, as this helps me to concentrate on what I am about to do.

Picture the Goddess and the God actually being present with you, and imagine them moving through the area, smelling and touching the plants. When you can see this clearly in your mind's eye, call upon them saying:

'I welcome the Lord and Lady to this place, which I have planted and tended in their honour.'

Next, complete your reserved task saying:

'As I take this last step towards completing this space, may they witness my care for the land and all living.'

As you finish this last step, say:

'Blessed Be.'

Now take the water in its vessel and, holding it in both hands, say:

'I call upon the Goddess and the God to bless and consecrate this water, may they nourish and care for this place, even as this water nourishes these plants.'

Sprinkle a little onto all the plants in your space and then say:

'Blessed Be.'

Next take the wine, or fruit juice, hold it up to the Goddess and the God and say:

'May the Lord and Lady bless and consecrate this wine. May they continue to guard, guide and protect me, even as they do so for the earth and all that lives upon it. Blessed Be.'

Take a sip of the wine and pour a little on the earth. Don't pour it too close to a growing plant, as it won't drink fruit juice or alcohol! If you are doing this for an indoor area, you might like to take a drop or two on the tips of your fingers and just transfer it to the soil. Thank the Goddess and the God by saying:

'I give thanks to the Goddess and the God for being with me. May I ever walk in their ways. Blessed Be.'

Lastly, remain and contemplate your space, perhaps finishing the rest of the drink.

CONTINUING CARE

Unlike the Sacred Space described in the preceding chapter, there are no particular times when you are more likely to use your area of contemplation. It could be daily, monthly or whenever you feel the need. As a result you will not have a lunar- or calendar-driven reminder to tend it. As I use mine nearly every day, it is a simple matter to take a look around and tend to any small jobs there each time I visit it. This way there's rarely much that needs attention. If your visits are likely to be less frequent you may need to set yourself a regular date on which to check if there are things which need tidying, watering, weeding, pruning, etc. However, in common with the Sacred Space you should always remember to call upon the Goddess and the God when working on the area, and let them guide you and aid your efforts.

USING THE SPACE

Having created a quiet and tranquil part of your garden there is no limit to the ways you might use it. As mentioned before it can simply be a place where you go to take a few breaths of air and to set yourself up for the day. It might be a place of refuge where you leave behind the hectic technological world, a sanctuary from TV, the phone and the computer! Mine is a place where I remind myself daily that the Goddess and the God are all around us and that the earth is the true home of the Craft. But there are other, more formal things you can do.

Meditation and pathworking are two techniques Witches use to draw closer to the Goddess and the God, and to seek the answers to questions. Meditation is a technique of stilling the mind by focussing on a single item or concept, and a space dedicated to the Gods is an excellent place for this. Pathworking is a form of guided meditation whereby you follow a story to a deity or destination where you are given the opportunity to ask a question and receive guidance; again your area is ideal for this.

An area dedicated to the Goddess and the God is special in its own right and, if private enough, a place to perform a self-blessing. The Rite of Self-Blessing can be performed whenever you feel tired, frustrated or just in need of a lift of the spirits. Those of you who have read my other books may already be familiar with a version of it, but for those of you who haven't, please read on.

Take a small bowl with some water into your area. Bless the water by drawing an invoking Pentagram [see Chapter 5, page 43] **in it with the forefinger of your strong hand and saying:**

'I do bless and consecrate this water in the name of the Mother Goddess. Blessed Be.'

Kneel and visualize the Goddess as Mother standing in front of you. Hold her image in your mind and say:

'Bless me Mother for I am your child.'

Dip your forefinger in the water and anoint your feet saying:

'Blessed Be my feet, that shall walk in thy ways.'

Anoint your knees, saying:

'Blessed Be my knees, that shall kneel at the sacred altar.'

Anoint just above your pubic bone and say:

'Blessed Be my womb (or phallus if you are male), that brings forth life.'

Anoint your chest, both sides and say:

'Blessed Be my breast, formed in beauty and in strength.'

Anoint your lips and say:

'Blessed Be my lips, that shall utter the sacred names.'

Anoint your nose and say:

'Blessed Be my nose, that shall breathe the sacred essence.'

Anoint your eyes and say:

'Blessed Be my eyes, that shall see thy ways.'

Anoint your forehead and say:

'Blessed Be my mind, that seekest understanding.'

Now visualize the Goddess reaching out and taking you in her arms. Wrap your own arms around yourself and say:

'Bless me Mother, for I am thy child. Blessed Be.'

Remain where you are for a few moments and feel the love, compassion and understanding of the Goddess enfolding you. When you feel ready, rise and clear away after yourself.

Your place dedicated to the Goddess and the God can also be used for spells and other magics. Often, if I am troubled, or have magic to work for others, I will also take the time to light a small candle in her area. A nightlight in a jam jar, to protect it from the wind and the plants from the flame, is ideal for this. I also make a point of going there at least once a month just to offer my thanks for everything which has been given me. It can be easy to turn to the Old Gods when you need something, but to forget all that they have already given you; the heat and light of the sun, the energy of the moon, your family, friends, health, hearth and home.

A SPELL TO BRING PEACE AND TRANQUILLITY INTO YOUR LIFE

Having an outdoor refuge is all very well, but sometimes all is not well in other parts of our lives. It could be problems within a relationship, either in the home or with others outside of it. Perhaps it is a problem with our workmates, or those of our partner, or perhaps someone else you care for has a problem in their environment.

Prior to working your magic, gather and carefully dry, or purchase, some white rose petals, jasmine flowers and lavender heads. Also find a small attractive dish to place these in. Before your spell take care to ensure that your area has been weeded and generally tidied, especially by removing any dead flower heads.

At the time of the Full Moon, although not necessarily at night, take your flowers to your quiet place, taking care that they cannot be swept away by the wind. Also take a white candle, or nightlight, in a jar to prevent it being blown out by any wind. Light the candle and perform the Self-Blessing as above. Then, whilst still kneeling, take the flowers and say:

'Great Mother of us all, I call upon you and your consort the God to give your blessings to all who are dear to me. Infuse these flowers with your love, that they bring patience, tolerance, calmness and peace to all who come near to them. Let their essence be as your essence. Blessed Be.'

Place the flowers in their chosen bowl, taking care to also place one of each beside the candle as an offering to the Gods saying:

'I leave these few in token of my love of the Old Gods and in thanks for all they give and have given to me. May my labours in this place also be an offering of thanks and may the Old Gods ever guard, guide and protect me and all who are in my thoughts. Blessed Be.'

Remain a few moments and meditate on all those you care for, whether family, friends or pets, before clearing away. If you are certain that the candle will be safe, you can leave it in place to burn down, otherwise take it into the house with you and burn it for as long as you can supervise it. Take the bowl of dried flowers and place it either centrally in your home, or in the room of the person you are working the magic for.

Not every Witch feels a close association with the Gods as personalities. Some feel that in the natural world they are so inherent in the land and in the Elements that these are the aspects they prefer to relate to. The next chapter focuses more on these aspects in the garden.

FIVE

THE ELEMENTAL
GARDEN

In the Craft the term 'Elements' is not used to mean rain, snow, wind or other aspects of the weather, it refers to the five Elements of Air, Fire, Water, Earth and Spirit. And these in turn are not simply references to things outside of us; they are a part of ourselves and are linked to all things.

⭐ Air is our thoughts, and as such should be the first part we invoke when preparing to do anything. Air is given the east quarter of the compass or Circle. Air also represents morning, Spring, youth and the first steps in any action. Air is often represented by the colour yellow, by incense or music. The plants linked to Air are those which have sound and movement like tall grasses, those which are highly scented and those with yellow flowers and foliage, although not because they are dying back!

⭐ Fire is our passions and enthusiasms, it is the part of us which is sparked to make a thought something we really want to carry out. Fire is the south quarter. Fire represents midday and the afternoon, Summer, adulthood and parenthood. Fire is often represented by the colour red, by candles, lights and the Sun. The plants of Fire are those with red flowers and foliage, in particular those with flame shapes like the red-hot poker.

⭐ Water is our emotions, that part of us which laughs, cries and becomes personally involved. Water is the west quarter. Water represents early evening, Autumn, maturity and the hopes and fears of personal involvement. Water is often represented by the colour blue, by shells and things of the sea and of course by water itself. The plants which represent Water are those which flourish in moist conditions, even though you may be growing them in a drier soil, such as willow and reeds, and of course those with blue flowers, or bluish foliage.

✦ Earth is the physical realm, our bodies, it marks the step of making things solid and 'real'. Earth is the north quarter, sometimes known as the place of power, the direction from which the Gods arrive. Earth represents evening, Winter, age and wisdom. Earth is represented by the colour green, or sometimes brown, by salt, and by rocks. All plants except those which grow on others, are linked to Earth, as this is the medium in which they grow. However, the plants most strongly linked are many of those with poisonous properties like nightshade, monkshood, wormwood and so on. Trees also, especially those which are native to your land, are more evocative of Earth. For me this includes oak, ash, elm, yew and many others, not all of which are suitable for the smaller garden.

✦ Spirit is the Goddess and the God and is the inner essence of ourselves. It is the thing which makes each of us uniquely who we are. Spirit has no direction as it is in all things at all times, yet it is also the centre of the Circle. Spirit can be represented by the colour violet or electric blue, and also by the purest white and the deepest black. In the Circle we ourselves represent and are Spirit, as are the Goddess and God upon whom we call. The plants of spirit are those whose scents have mood-enhancing properties, like lavender, rosemary, jasmine, honeysuckle and so on. Night-flowering plants are considered closely linked to Spirit, such as night-scented stocks, some jasmines, and so on.

Of course the directions attributed to the Elements above are those of the Circle. When they are applied to the Pentagram each has its own point. If you visualize a Pentagram placed over a clock face with a single point at 12 then the following can be used to give you an idea: Earth is placed at approximately 7, Air at 9, Fire at 5, Water at 3 and Spirit at 12 (see diagram on page 40).

In the Craft we draw energy from the Elements both within and without to create our magic. It is an essential part of every Witch's development to be able to bring their internal Elements into balance so that they do not approach their work with one or more in dominance over the others. Magic approached in an unbalanced way will be

less effective or will fail altogether. An Elemental garden should provide a space where it becomes easier to balance the energies and a place where it is possible to recharge your inner 'batteries'. If daily life has been hectic and full of stress you may feel the need to focus more on the Elements of Air and Spirit, for example, and if it seems dull and flat then it may be that you need more Fire and Water in your make-up. Simply tending an Elemental garden can help to bring your energies back into balance, and working your magic there will benefit from having a natural balance in and around you.

As you can see, there is more to an Elemental garden than simply taking the climate or weather into account, although these must be considered when any kind of planting takes place. However magical your plans, you cannot ignore the prevailing conditions or your plants will not flourish. The Elements in their raw state, so to speak, are present in every garden, whether large or just a couple of pots. Plants grow in the earth. They need light and warmth (Fire), and Water. They photosynthesize with Air, and each has its own Spirit as well as your own Spirit, in the form of the care you take of them. But there are many ways you can bring out the Elemental qualities to make yours a truly Elemental garden.

PLANNING YOUR ELEMENTAL GARDEN

There are aspects of planning an Elemental garden which are similar to those in creating an outdoor Sacred Space, but as you are not constrained to creating a working area, the Elemental garden can also be far more freeform. In fact, unless you choose to be very overt, no one other than yourself need be aware that your garden is in any way 'Witchy'!

Probably the easiest way to bring out the Elements is by planting according to direction and colour. Thus plants in the east would be yellow, those in the south red and so on. It does not even have to be all plants in each direction of a particular colour, which might look a little contrived; for your purposes it may be enough to have just one or two. Certainly, if you are creating your garden in a small space, or even indoors, then one plant for each Element will be sufficient.

One of the nicer ideas I have seen was confined to a small circular bed. An inner circle of purple (in this case lavender) was surrounded by four quarter arcs of yellow (wood sage and toadflax), red (poppies and red clover), green (parsley and witch grass) and blue (cornflowers and bluebells). The delineating lines between the different segments, as well as the outer edge of the circle were made of small pieces of coloured stones collected from beaches around the country. Part of the charm of this for me was that each stone, and many of the plants themselves, held memories of happy trips spent foraging for the parts. This one small piece of garden became a sort of living scrapbook of good times as well as an Elemental garden.

Each of the Elements also has its own symbol. In some magical systems these are a series of triangles: Air being an upright triangle with a horizontal line across it; Fire an upright triangle without a line; Water a downward-pointing triangle with no line; Earth a downward-pointing triangle with a line across, and Spirit a wheel with eight spokes. An alternative system gives Air a circle, Fire a downward-pointing triangle, Water a crescent with the 'horns' pointing upwards and Earth a square. Spirit is repre-sented by an upright oval. If you wish you can incorporate either of these systems into your design, perhaps placing plants in these shapes within a border or borders.

The Elements do not have to be represented either by plants or the shape of your planting, indeed this may not be possible within an existing garden. Garden ornaments with appropriate themes can be utilized: these days there are many ornamental statues, plaques and planters available. You could even make your own, either from scratch or by painting emblems and symbols onto bought ones. Birds or feathers can be used for Air, flames for Fire, shells for Water, tree shapes for Earth, and for Spirit you might like to have a statue of the Goddess or one of the many Green Man plaques which are popular these days.

An alternative is to incorporate symbols of the Elements as a part of the structure of your garden. Borders can be delineated using either shapes or objects representing the Elements: feathery shapes for Air, flame-like ones for Fire and so on.

Another idea which we have considered in our garden is to dig a sunken circle, using the removed earth to build up a circular bank around it, with a break in the circle which will be used to gain access to the circle. This will give us a space 6 inches (15 cm) below the normal soil level, but over a foot below the level of the bank. I'm hoping that this will also have the secondary effect of protecting the area from stray footballs, etc! Into the bank at each quarter we propose to set a flat stone, large enough to be used as a seat,

but also able to take Elemental symbols should we wish to work magic there. The plants around each of these 'seats' will also be symbolic of the four Elements, and tall enough to provide a gentle screen. In the centre of the circle we will erect a small purple slate 'monolith' (if that's not a contradiction in terms), about 18 inches (46 cm) high, to represent Spirit. It is worth noting that any tall stones must be set in deep enough to be secure – usually a quarter to a third of their height needs to be underground.

INVOKING THE ELEMENTS AND SEEKING THE BLESSING OF THE GODDESS AND THE GOD

As mentioned earlier, the Elements are present in the garden at all times, but it is worth taking the extra steps to make your garden special for you. Having decided how you wish to incorporate Elemental features, but before you actually commence work, take the time to perform the following small Ritual. If you can, perform this on a day and at a time when you will immediately be able to make at least a token start on your gardening work.

You will need to collect some rainwater in the period of the Waxing Moon and create an asperger as detailed in Chapter 3. At the Full Moon take your water and asperger into the centre of the area. Holding up the water, visualize the Goddess and the God and call upon them:

'I call upon the Goddess and the God, Mother and Father of all life, to be with me in this place of growing. I ask that they lend their energies and that they do bless this water as a symbol of the energies of life and living. Blessed Be.'

Now take the water to each of the places you have chosen for each of the Elements, starting with Air. Using your asperger sprinkle some of the water in the shape of an invoking Pentagram of that element. For Air this means (using the 'clock face' as a template) starting at 3, moving to 9, then 5, then 12, then 7 and finally returning to 3. As you draw each invoking Pentagram call upon that Element:

'I call upon the Element of Air, from the gentle breeze which cools in the Summer Sun, to the strong wind which clears away the fallen leaves. Each in its turn and in its season, be present in this place, and cast your Blessings on this land. Blessed Be.'

Using your asperger sprinkle some of the water in the shape of an invoking Pentagram of Fire in the following sequence: 12, 5, 9, 3, 7, 12.

'I call upon the Element of Fire, the light and heat of the Sun from the short Winter days which allow rest, to the long hot Summer ones which inspire growth. Each in its turn and in its season, be present in this place, and cast your Blessings on this land. Blessed Be.'

Using your asperger sprinkle some of the water in the shape of an invoking Pentagram of Water in the following sequence: 9, 3, 7, 12, 5, 9.

'I call upon the Element of Water, from the gentle showers of Spring, to the heavy rains which revitalize the land. Each in its turn and in its season, be present in this place, and cast your Blessings on this land. Blessed Be.'

Using your asperger sprinkle some of the water in the shape of an invoking Pentagram of Earth in the following sequence: 12, 7, 3, 9, 5, 12.

'I call upon the Element of Earth, the substance of our world and the soil from which all rises; the Earth in which the seeds sprout, the plants grow, and which gives Winter rest. Each in its turn and in its season, give your strengths to this place, and cast your Blessings here. Blessed Be.'

For Spirit draw the eight-spoked wheel.

'I call upon the Goddess and the God, from whom all life rises and to whom all must return, who set the pace and time of the seasons, be present in this place, and cast your Blessings on this land. Blessed Be.'

Now put any remaining water and your asperger to one side and commence work on your area. When you have finished for the day, or for this period, thank the Goddess and the God:

'I give thanks to the Goddess and the God. May their Blessings ever remain on this place and upon all who tend and come to it. Blessed Be.'

Normally, when you invoke the Elements for Ritual or magic you would thank and dismiss them afterwards. However, here you are invoking them in their natural state to a natural place, and are, if you like, simply making more formal and bringing into balance an existing presence. Therefore you do not need, or want, to dismiss them.

DEDICATING YOUR ELEMENTAL GARDEN

As with the other forms of garden your Elemental garden is dedicated by you as you work on it. In this case though, you need to call upon the Elements as well as the Goddess and the God.

Each time you commence work recite the following:

'Earth my body, Water my blood, Air my breath, and Fire my spirit.
Lord and Lady, come to me, be with me, mark my work and lend your energy.'

Whilst you do so, visualize each of the Elements as well as the Goddess and the God. You may find that this takes some practice, but it is well worth it as this is also a way of balancing your energies. Also, as a chant/mantra it can be used whenever you feel the need to harness your own energy to address troubles in other aspects of your life.

CONSECRATING YOUR ELEMENTAL GARDEN

In blessing and dedicating the garden you invoked the Elements and the Goddess and the God. When Consecrating it you will need to place the emphasis on the balance between the Elements as this is an area you will be using primarily for personal balance, in addition to relaxation and magic. Because of this the ideal time to perform this Ritual would be at either the Spring, or Autumn, Equinox when the energies of the Wheel of the Year are in balance. Having said that, if either Equinox is some way off you do not need to wait, instead perform the Ritual during the Waxing Moon close to, but not on, the Full Moon so that you are making the most of the build up of Lunar energy.

Prior to your Ritual save one piece of trimmed back old or dead foliage and one healthy cutting or shoot for planting, feeding or watering; something new. Take with you into your space a chalice and some wine or fruit juice. Also take some incense (an incense stick is fine) and something to burn it safely in or on, a night-light or candle (in a jar to protect it from the wind), some water and a little salt. Don't forget some matches to light the candle and incense! Place all these in a central, but convenient, part of your space.

    Light the candle and incense. Invoke the quarters and invite the Goddess and the God as you did when Blessing the Garden, above. Now settle yourself down, sitting is probably best. Calm your breathing and focus on the land around you. Take time to appreciate the sights, sounds and scents around you, as well as the feel of the earth beneath you.

    Now close your eyes and visualize the Goddess holding a set of scales, the kind where two separate bowls balance each other. Now visualize yourself

placing each Elemental part of yourself in turn into one of the bowls, followed by the God placing its natural equivalent in the other. For example, you place the Air of your thoughts in one bowl, then the God places the natural Element of Air into the other, and so on with Fire, Water and Earth. Then place your Spirit into your bowl visualizing it as a sphere of bluish purple light. When you have done so, watch as the Goddess and the God together place a similar sphere into the other bowl. Now visualize the scales balancing, and keep doing so until they appear totally level. Still using visualization ask the Goddess and the God to hold and maintain your balance in their care and trust, and to pour it into the earth of your garden. Watch as they tip both sides of the scales into the land. When they have done so, give them your thanks and then open your eyes.

Now perform your last acts of removing the old (trimming away) and creating the new (planting or watering) and say:

'With this act of removing the old and nurturing the new I make my bond of balance in this place. I will tend and care for all living here, that the balance thus shown be reflected in myself and my life. Blessed Be.'

Take the wine, or juice, and hold it before you and say:

'I call upon the Old Gods to bless this fruit of the land. As they bring life and balance to all things living, let them extend that life and balance to this place, to me and to all who come here. May their presence ever be here, holding the Elements in balance and the magic of the earth in their hands.'

You might like to take a moment to visualize yourself, your family, friends and even pets, moving into and through the area and being happy, contented and in balance. Take a sip of the wine, or juice, and say:

'Blessed Be.'

Now sprinkle a little of the wine around your area, remembering to move deosil (clockwise) at all times. As you do so say:

'*As the Goddess and the God have blessed this wine, let it represent their blessings on the earth and all life. Blessed Be.*'

Thank the Elements, the Goddess and the God as you did for the Blessing above. Remain for a while and enjoy the feeling of your area before clearing away after yourself.

CONTINUING CARE OF YOUR ELEMENTAL GARDEN

As balance is the theme and key to an Elemental garden you will need to keep an eye on the different plants or zones, so that they are literally kept in balance. This may mean that some plants need regular cutting back. Others may need more encouragement or you may need to supplement an Element by adding a further plant or plants. It is worth observing the growth patterns of the different Elements as often we can gain insights into the balance of ourselves and our lives from the way they are growing. If the Fire plant or zone is vigorous and thriving, you may find that passion is beginning to come to the fore in your life. You can then use this knowledge to address inner problems. Having said that, it is also important to bear in mind the physical preferences of the plants themselves, e.g. your 'Air' plants may not be doing well due to a pest problem, rather than a lack of thought in your life!

The best times for tending an Elemental garden are the first and third quarters of the Moon, the times when it appears to be a half circle in the sky. These are the centres of the waxing and waning periods and the time when it is seen as neither more, nor less illuminated than dark. However, any major pruning or redesign work is best under-taken at the Spring and Autumn Equinoxes, rather than in a part of the Lunar cycle. Whenever you wish to use your Elemental garden, and whenever you work on it, take a few moments to examine the Elemental balance, or lack of it, within you. In this way you will be able to focus on whichever Elements within you which are not in balance, before letting the garden work it's magic on you.

USING YOUR ELEMENTAL GARDEN

There are two key aspects to using an Elemental garden: one is to seek and maintain inner balance to help you in daily life, the other is to take that balance into your magic. As the Elements are probably the single most important key to successful magic, this is an ideal space for spellcraft. Here you are regularly working on maintaining a balance between the Elements and here you will find it most easy to balance your own energies, which is fundamental if you are to be able to draw on the energies of the Elements outside.

Whenever you think, or even suspect, that your energies might not be balanced, take the time to go to your Elemental garden and work on it. This will have the effect of helping you to clear all the surface clutter in your mind, such as what to cook for tea or what to wear tomorrow, and enabling you to consider carefully what is really happening in your life. Are you spending too much time in thought, perhaps making plans, so that little progress is really actually made? Perhaps you have had a number of disagreements with those close to you – is this because your inner Fire is dominant? As mentioned above, sometimes the growth patterns of the plants themselves will give you a hint. Once you feel that you have identified the unbalanced Element, do not immediately start work to 'correct' it, but give some thought to why this might be. Are other people's demands putting pressure on a particular Elemental aspect? Is this a seasonal effect? For example, many people find that Fire seems to dominate in very hot weather. Once you have identified not only the unbalanced Element(s) but also the likely cause, then you will be in a position not only to re-balance your Elements but also to address the root cause in an effective way.

To rebalance your energies, stand barefoot in the centre of your Elemental area. Close your eyes and take several deep, slow breaths to focus yourself. Now, feel the ground beneath your feet, wriggle your toes, really come into contact with it and focus the whole of your mind on how it feels. Next, take some more deep breaths, focusing on the air entering your lungs and chest, think about it being taken up by your bloodstream and circulated around your whole body. Now think about the blood itself, the liquid that moves through your veins to nourish you, just as streams and rivers carry water around the land. Think about your heart, the great pump and engine of the body, the source of heat and energy, just as the Sun is for the Earth. Lastly, think about the inner spark of self, which is you and is your Spirit. Remember that the Goddess and the God are also Spirit, and because of this they are within you, as well as all around. Take a few moments to reflect on this, for that spark of Spirit within you is a pale echo of the Spirit all around. Keep breathing slowly and deeply until you can feel the Elements within you moving and adjusting back to the balance which is yours naturally. When you are ready, open your eyes and take a moment to return fully to the here and now. Take a further few moments to look around the Elemental garden and to tend to any tasks which need doing. Whilst you are doing this, remember to thank the Goddess and the God and each of the Elements for the calm which they have brought you. You can also request their help in addressing the root cause of your imbalance. When you have finished in the garden make sure that you actually take the first steps towards making any necessary change.

A SPELL FOR THE PROMOTION OF NATURE'S PEST KILLERS IN YOUR GARDEN

Many gardeners forget that, although some insects, birds and animals may do damage in the garden, there are others which are helpful. Many of the garden pests we try to eliminate have natural enemies and they can do the job far more successfully than we can.

For this spell you will need some fallen wood; if your area is large then several logs, if it is small then perhaps just a couple of small pieces. If you are growing plants inside only, then you need just a small token piece, perhaps an inch or so in length. The wood should have either fallen naturally or have been cut as part of a woodland maintenance plan, and if it has had the chance to lie for a few months, so much the better. Do not cut or tear branches off living trees, or use wood which has been chemically treated in any way, including being painted. Unless you are only growing plants indoors, do not clean your wood in any way, keep it as close to the state in which you found it as possible.

This spell is best worked at the Full Moon, for you will be drawing on the energies of growth from the waxing period as well as the energies of banishment from the waning period. It is also best worked at dawn or dusk, when day and night are in flux.

Place the wood in the centre of your Elemental space, and kneel beside it. Placing both forefingers on it, call upon each of the Elements in turn whilst visualizing the actions you are describing:

'I call upon the Element of Air. May the winds send things living to remove all pests and drive disease from this place. Blessed Be.

'I call upon the Element of Fire. May the Sun give life to all things which promote the life and growth of this place. Blessed Be.

'I call upon the Element of Water. May the rains wash away all that might cause harm to the life in this place. Blessed Be.

'I call upon the Element of Earth. Give succour to the good and no place to the bad in this place. Blessed Be.'

Now remove your hands and hold them palms down above the wood, visualizing the Goddess and the God:

'I call upon the Goddess and the God to send their Blessing into this haven for all that which promotes the health of the land. Lend your strength and support to all of your creations which cleanse and protect the life in this place.'

Lower your palms onto the wood and visualize the energy of the Old Gods flowing from all around and passing through you down into the wood. When you are sure this has taken place say:

'Blessed Be.'

Now pick up your piece or pieces of wood and find a sheltered, but not overly wet, part of your garden and place your wood there. If your Elemental garden is pot plants in the house then place it on the soil of the plant which most likes damp soil. In either case leave it undisturbed to Rot In Peace!

Once your wood has been placed, thank each of the Elements, the Goddess and the God in turn.

Not only is this a magical remedy, but fallen wood really does attract the kind of beetles and insects which help to keep pests under control. If you have a very large garden you might wish to repeat this process so that you have logs or branches in several parts to maximize the amount of pest control. There are other suggestions for natural protection and elimination in Chapter 11.

SIX

THE GARDEN OF SPELLS AND MAGIC

Of course you do not have to use your garden as a place for working magic, it can be made up of the magical works, or spells, themselves. Sometimes it is easy to get caught up in the idea that magical tools and the components for spells come from shops, and to forget that the most magical things are growing all around us. It as is a result of the society in which we live that we assume that money has to change hands to make a thing of value or use. But if you consider it carefully, will a crystal that was ripped out of the earth with explosives and prepared using underpaid child labour have any magical properties left in it? But the planting and tending of a single seed can be the central part of your spell.

Outside of the Craft, plants and flowers are often used as the physical expression of non-physical concepts; a pot plant to say thank you, a bunch of flowers to say sorry, planting a tree as a living memorial to a loved one or to welcome a new child. All these are in their own way small acts of magic – hopes and wishes, as it were, expressed in living form. In earlier centuries, specific flowers and plants were given specific meanings, the language of flowers. As Witches we can take this further, we can select the plant most suitable for our magic and plant it as the magical act itself. This has the happy side effect of not leaving you with a completed spell to be disposed of when the magic has worked, as you can just let a plant continue to grow. Not only that, but if you are working for someone unsympathetic to Wiccan, Pagan or even just 'New Age' ideas, they are much more likely to appreciate a plant than a crystal, talisman or other item which fits neither their décor nor their life style!

Not only can your garden be made of the magics you have worked, it can also be made up of, or include, your way of paying for the magics you work. A great many people forget that magic and spells should be paid for, and not just successful magic, all magic. You should always do something to recompense the energies you draw on, whether you used and directed them properly, or wasted them. Obviously, you cannot repay the Elements, the Goddess and the God with money, although there are some spells which require the use of a coin. Some Witches feel that payment is made in the form of libations of wine and food, poured onto the earth. Others feel that you should offer something of value: perfume, oil or even a precious object. Whilst either of these views is valid, I feel that our payments, just like our sacrifices, should take the form of time and energy expended. Whilst I realize that anything of value which you offer represents the effort you put into earning the money to purchase it, I still feel that it is more in keeping with the nature-based foundation of the Craft if your payment directly benefits the land and all that lives on it. Those of you who have read my other books may recall suggestions to go litter-collecting on your local green space, thoughts on recycling and cautions about littering pre-historic monuments with dead flowers and other offerings. As Witches I feel it is important that we try to walk lightly on the land and actively contribute to its wellbeing as it is the heart of our beliefs and lives.

PLANNING A SPELL GARDEN

Unlike the uses referred to in the previous chapters, a garden where the plants are living spells need not contain a particular area devoted to your Craft. You can plant your spells in amongst your existing layout, perhaps adding an extra plant to an existing group. No one is likely to question an additional snowdrop in an existing group, or another clump of lavender on the end of an existing bank of it. You can keep within any current scheme of, say, all red and pink plants in one area. Alternatively, you could plant spells into any of the other designs in this book. The Witch with little or no outside space may find this technique a simpler alternative too as, considerations of heat and light aside, this means that plants can live wherever there is the space to put them: windowsills, floors, the tops of furniture, etc. Furthermore, just as a talisman is given to the person for whom the magic was worked, so too can a plant be handed on to the spell's recipient.

Having said that, some Witches like to keep a special place in the garden where the plant, particularly one in a pot, stays for a certain period of time. This period could be three days and nights, which is the usual timescale for setting a spell in action. It is also a sensible amount of time to give a new plant time to settle into its new home, a sort of intensive-care period. Alternatively, the plant may stay in its special place until the magic has worked and then it is transferred to a more permanent site.

Of course you can apply a more formal pattern and actually create a Spell Garden. I know of one where the planting areas have been divided into 12 roughly equal zones. Each of these has then been given its own sign of the zodiac. When the owner wants to work magic for someone she will either plant in the zone of that person's sign, or where that is unknown, in the zone closest to the nature of the magic. This idea could also be adapted for planetary zones.

WORKING PLANT SPELLS

Plant spells are extremely good for kinds of magic which involve growth, development and changes which are ongoing, such as study, work, career, health, relationships, family and home. They are not useful for 'instant' magics, like finding that car parking space! As with all magics you need to start by thinking carefully about the purpose of the spell and the person for whom you are working it. You also need to give careful thought to which plant you will be using.

Plants can be selected according to their relevance to the person; you might choose one of their favourite species, or one associated with their Sun sign. Alternatively, you could select by their association with the problem you are addressing (there's a list further on in this chapter and references to many helpful books in Appendix III). However, you will also need to take into account the following: What are the plant's natural requirements, in terms of heat and light, etc? What are its physical properties – will it grow too tall or run rampant? Is it acceptable? Not everyone is happy to plant nettles or brambles in the garden, let alone have them in a pot in the house, no matter how magical they may be!

Generally speaking, plant spells are best performed during the Waxing Moon, and either in the early morning or late afternoon. There is no need to work this kind of magic at night; not only will you look a bit odd doing your gardening when it's dark, but plants prefer gentle light after the trauma of a move. Another consideration is where you will actually perform your spell. It really is better to perform plant magic outside, after all that is the natural environment for it and there will almost certainly be a messy element involved! If you really cannot go outside, then choose a location where it is possible to minimize the mess caused by spillage of soil and water. In the following example of a plant spell I have assumed you will be putting your plant into a pot (purchased plants usually need to be moved up a pot size as soon as possible), but if you are keeping it at home, then it could just as easily go into the ground.

A PLANT SPELL RITUAL

Having carefully selected your time and place, considered the problem and decided which plant to use, you should collect together everything you will need. Remember to include in your 'magical equipment' soil, a pot, a trowel or digging implement, water and so on. I prefer to keep separate 'gardening' tools for this sort of work as many of my spells are smaller plants intended to be given away, and conventional tools are too cumbersome. Mine are an old teaspoon, dessertspoon and fork, all bought from second-hand shops. In addition, I have a small plastic bottle with a 'sports cap' which is ideal for gently watering around the plant, without getting leaves and flowers wet.

Make yourself comfortable and take several deep breaths to centre yourself. Close your eyes and invoke the Elements in turn, visualizing them and saying:

'I call upon the Element of Air (Fire, Water, Earth), join with me and lend your power today.'

When you feel that Element's presence say:

'Blessed Be.'

Now visualize the Goddess and the God:

'I call upon the Goddess and the God. Mother and Father of all living, in whose hands all nature lies, be with me here and lend your power that I might help … (name of person).'

Again, when you feel their presence say:

'Blessed Be.'

Now take a few moments to focus on the person you are working for, the nature of their problem, and the outcome you desire for them. Remove the plant from its existing container, place a little soil into the base of the new pot and, just before you add the plant, say:

'May gentle winds breathe life into this … (name of plant), that it may help … (name of person) to … (name the desired outcome). Blessed Be.

'May the light and warmth of the Sun give life unto this … (name of plant), that it may help … (name of person) to … (name the desired outcome). Blessed Be.

'May gentle rains sprinkle life unto this … (name of plant), that it may help … (name of person) to … (name the desired outcome). Blessed Be.

'May the Earth itself nourish and give life unto this … (name of plant), that it may help … (name of person) to … (name the desired outcome). Blessed Be.'

Place the plant into its new home, add any extra soil required to make it fit and then water in. Once your potting is complete, wipe around the outside of the new container to make it clean. Now, holding it in both hands, visualize the Goddess and the God again, and say:

'I call upon the Goddess and the God to bring life and health to this … (name of plant). May it thrive and grow. May it bring healing and happiness to … (name of the person). Blessed Be.'

Still holding the plant in both hands, focus as strongly as you can and visualize the energies of the Elements, the Goddess and the God, being poured into it from all around. Imagine it is being filled with gold and silver particles of life. When you feel that it cannot contain any more, place it on the ground again.

Once again visualize each of the Elements in turn and say:

'I give thanks to the Element of Air (Fire, Water, Earth) for your help today, and for your continuing part in the life of our world. Blessed Be.'

Visualize the Goddess and the God and say:

'Gracious Mother and Father of all life and all living, I give thanks to you for lending your power and for the cycles of life, death and rebirth which sustain the ever-renewing life of this land. Blessed Be.'

Put the plant in its appointed place and tidy away after yourself.

PLANTS FOR SPELLS AND MAGIC

The following are some examples of the kinds of problem you might want to address and the plants you could use for them. It is by no means an exhaustive list as every plant, herb, tree and shrub has magical properties of one kind or another. I have a dozen books on plants and their attributions and still find new ideas to try. Chapter 10 lists some plants for magical work and Appendix III gives the titles of some useful books.

Concentration, study, knowledge:	Basil, bay, lemon balm, clover, eyebright, lily of the valley, all types of mint, sage, rosemary, rue. The presence of a rosemary plant close to a work or study area is very beneficial as the scent of its leaves encourages clear thought and concentration.
Work, career, prosperity and success:	Cinquefoil, honesty, lemon balm, marigold, moss, orange, rowan, St John's wort, snapdragon, sunflower, tulip. Golden flowers are considered to attract the power of the Sun and success.
Wisdom:	Broom, dandelion, goldenrod, iris, meadowsweet, sage. The latter is an example of the way in which the old names for plants often reflected their use.
To attract luck and good fortune:	Bluebell, clover, daffodil, fern, heather, holly, moss, myrtle, strawberry. Contrary to popular myth it is the five-leafed clover which attracts luck, four leaves being protective.
Health and healing:	Angelica, bay, blackberry, cowslip, cranberry, fennel, garlic, hops, lavender, rosemary, rowan, sorrel, violet. A great many plants have healing properties, some magical, others physical. The few I have selected here are for general magical healing – being included here does not necessarily mean you can eat them!

Friendship and relationships:	Cyclamen, daisy, forget-me-not, hyacinth, lemon, myrtle, passionflower, rose, sweet pea, tansy. The giving of almost any nice plant is a good way to cement a friendship, whether with magical intention or not, as the giver is usually remembered every time the plant is tended. However, it is important to select something which is going to please, rather than something which turns out to be a nuisance. I was the recipient of a rather large and decidedly aggressive cactus once, and after receiving several wounds from it I felt less than enamoured of the giver!
To attract romance, love, partnerships:	Bachelor's buttons, columbine, honeysuckle, maidenhair, passionflower, plum, sweet pea, valerian. Growing columbine and honeysuckle each side of the door and training them to meet over it is considered to strengthen and maintain the bonds between all those in the house. There's even a song about it!
Fertility:	Carrot, daffodil, damiana, dock, fig, geranium, gooseberry, grape, hawthorn, mistletoe, oak, poppy, raspberry, wheat. The influence of grape is not confined to the plant – pictures of bunches of grapes over the bed were thought by the Romans to ensure conception.
Protection of home and family:	Angelica, foxglove, holly, hyacinth, ivy, larkspur, oak, parsley, primrose, rowan, thistle, wisteria, witch hazel, wolfs-bane. Hyacinth grown near the bed induces harmony and protects against nightmares. It's a good one to keep in a child's bedroom, once they are old enough to be trusted not to eat it!
To bring peace and harmony:	Catmint, damiana, gardenia, hops, jasmine, lavender, lilac, rose, valerian, verbena, violet. Both catmint and valerian are irresistible to some cats, so try to plant them where you don't mind feline visitors!

Enhancement of intuitive and psychic ability:

Bay, borage, broom, jasmine, lemongrass, mugwort, rowan, thyme, witch grass, wormwood.

A selection of the leaves and flowers of the above can be dried and sewn into a small cushion. Placed under your pillow it will enhance your abilities while you sleep.

CONTINUING CARE OF YOUR LIVING SPELLS

Some people feel a little nervous about the idea of growing their spells, in case the plant in question fails to grow, as they fear this indicates that the spell has failed. Whilst a perfectly healthy plant which dies the day after the magic may be an indicator that all was not well with either the spell itself or the intention behind the magic, in most cases a plant fails to thrive for more prosaic reasons, like damage, soil, light, heat, water, disease and pests. Obviously, when selecting a plant for magic, as for any other purpose, it's as well to choose one which looks healthy, preferably with signs of new growth occurring. However, observing the results of plant spells can sometimes give us interesting insights into our inner feelings about the sorts of magic we are working! For example, when a normally successful gardener plants a spell and then it suffers from, say, damage or lack of water, perhaps that gardener's heart was not in the spell in the first place. On the other hand, if you've never had any luck with, say, poppies, then it's probably a good idea not to use them for your living spells.

As mentioned above, three days and nights is a traditional period for the consolidation of a spell. It is also a good period for the nurturing of a new, or newly moved, plant. Therefore, it is excellent for the newly planted spell plant. In those first three days it is a good idea to visit the plant morning and evening to check whether is has enough water, and is not in either too much or too little light. But whilst this is sufficient on the magical side, it is not enough time to be sure that a plant is actually going to thrive. More subtle diseases and pests can take a lot longer to emerge, so if you are giving the plant away you will need to give it a couple of weeks before being sure of its physical health. If you are using seeds and the resulting plant is to be given to another, then you might prefer to wait until there really is a visible plant before handing it over!

SEVEN

THE MEDICINAL

GARDEN

The uses of plants are not confined to their magical qualities – a good many herbs and plants have medicinal properties. Indeed, it is these plants that most people think of when they think of a Witch's garden. The image of the Witch as herbal healer is not only traditional it is very accurate. It is, however, a lot less exciting than some people imagine.

A lot of people think that the plants of the Witch are those with the ability to change physical and mental awareness. However, any plant which achieves this will do so as an indicator that it is poisonous. Indeed, some are so toxic that simply handling them can cause severe illness and even death. Whilst it is true that any good herbalist would have known which plants induced visions, could make someone ill or even kill, this knowledge would have been used to avoid such effects. The Witch who poisoned 'clients' would soon have no clients! The reality is that Witches and other healers of the past would have used those plants which most safely and reliably solved the problems of those who came to them. The myth of the use of toxic compounds came about partly as a result of the Witch hunts, as it was an easy accusation to level at a time when illness and death were not well understood. Indeed, several historical outbreaks of malevolent 'Witchcraft' have now been proven to have been caused by toxic plants or compounds getting into the food supply, not by Witchcraft, but by carelessness and ignorance. The other reason was to discredit those (mostly female) healers who helped their community in exchange for the goods or services which were affordable, at the time when medicine started to become the preserve of a more formal (male) medical profession, who charged money for their treatments.

PLANTS HISTORICALLY ASSOCIATED WITH WITCHCRAFT

As interest in these plants is still prevalent I will include the better-known here, together with their likely effects. Whilst they do have medicinal applications these really are best left to the trained and qualified herbalist – you should certainly not be experimenting on your friends and family! Those marked * should not be grown in amongst plants destined for the kitchen and children should be kept well away.

Aconite (monkshood or wolfs-bane) *	A deadly poison which can be absorbed through the skin. Aconite causes a tingling sensation, numbness, nausea and a variety of unpleasant symptoms leading to death if an antidote is not supplied.
Belladonna (deadly nightshade) *	Highly poisonous in all its parts, belladonna can also be absorbed through cuts in the skin. It causes hallucinations, paralysis, coma and death.
Damiana	Damiana has long been reputed to have aphrodisiac powers. However, it can also induce nausea, will act as a diuretic and is extremely bitter. Whilst a relatively safe plant to grow, tinctures and tablets are readily available (at present), and are far safer as well as more pleasant to take.
Mistletoe *	The leaves and berries of mistletoe are poisonous if eaten, causing heart attacks, convulsions and death – even two or three can kill a child. Although marked *, as a parasitic plant usually growing high above ground, it is less dangerous than others, until picked and brought into the house.
Morning glory/Bindweed (Convolvulus Duartinus)	Morning glory seeds are reputed to induce visions, however they also induce nausea, interfere with the action of the liver and are extremely dangerous to the pregnant woman and her unborn child. As they are often commercially treated with mercury there are additional

dangers of mercuric poisoning with symptoms of vomiting, diarrhoea and liver damage. Furthermore, bindweed is something most of us strive to keep out of the garden as it is a prolific creeper and climber and has a tendency to take over and strangle other plants.

Skullcap (mad dogweed)

Skullcap is a tranquillizer, and has been used in a number of forms for calming and soothing those with convulsions. However, it can also cause giddiness, confusion, twitching and an irregular heartbeat.

Thorn Apple
(Datura stramonium, *jimson weed)**

Thorn apple is extremely poisonous, and warns potential browsing animals by giving off a foul smell and having a nauseous taste. It can be absorbed through cuts in the skin, or even by touching the eyes or mouth with hands which have touched the plant. It causes dilation of the pupil, dimness of sight, giddiness, delirium and can cause death.

Valerian

Valerian is a relatively safe herb in this category and is used to calm and soothe, as it has slight sedative properties. Valerian leaves can be soaked in cold water for 12 hours and then strained and drunk to aid sleep. I have even used a drop of valerian oil on my child's pillow to aid sleep from time to time. However, overuse, either in quantity or frequency, can cause depression, headaches and slow the heart. To gain the best results valerian can be used for one to two weeks, then there should be a break of equal length. It is worth noting that valerian has a strong smell which is very attractive to some cats who will roll on it and prevent it growing well.

Wormwood (Artemisia absinthium)

Once the principle ingredient in absinthe (a drink noted for causing blindness in regular users), the main uses of this herb are in treating flatulence and worms, hence the name! As it has a very unpleasant taste, even small amounts can cause nausea. Overuse of wormwood can cause dizziness, insomnia, nightmares and convulsions.

PLANTS FOR THE MEDICINAL GARDEN

There is a wide variety of plants that can be used medicinally but, unless you are planning to spend a lifetime studying them, have a very large garden and are proposing to treat a wide range of physical ills, you will not need or want to grow more than a handful of them. You will almost certainly be familiar with most of the plants in the following selection, as they are found in many a kitchen or garden. But, in addition to their ability to enhance the flavour of food, they also have medicinal qualities. In fact, it is likely that their healing properties led them to be regularly grown and subsequently incorporated into daily use.

One of the advantages of growing and using these better-known herbs is that their taste is much more acceptable to the palate. Whilst herbal medicines are, on the whole, safe to use, you can overdo it. It is best when starting out to try at most one or two 'doses' a day for a week, and then assess the results.

Angelica	Angelica root can be made into an infusion and used to treat coughs, colds, sore throat, hoarseness and bronchitis. It will also relieve flatulence and colic, and soothe an upset stomach. It should not be used by diabetics.
Basil	Sweet basil leaves can be gently crushed and smelt to alleviate headaches, nervousness and panic attacks. Made into a tea it cleanses the digestive system, helping to stop vomiting and reduce nausea, and was believed to stimulate

milk production in nursing mothers. Mixed with oil, basil
will relieve constipation. It has antiseptic properties and
can be used to bathe wounds or to add to a bath.

Bay
Bay, or laurel, leaves can be crushed and infused into a
weak tea which stimulates mind, body and appetite
(although you may need to sweeten it with honey). The
leaves can also be incorporated into a poultice or dressing
to relieve bruises, sprains and pain. Bay leaves can also be
carried, or hung in bunches around the house, to deter
flying insects.

Bergamot
Red bergamot flowers can be made into a pleasant tea
which soothes, relaxes and will aid sleep. They can also be
dried and added to a sleep sachet or pillow. Overuse may
cause the skin to become photosensitive.

Borage
Borage leaves can be added to cold drinks to provide a
mental and physical boost. Alternatively, steep some in
water and add a little lemon and sugar for a refreshing and
restorative drink. The blue star-shaped flowers are also
added to salads to give the flavours a 'lift', but don't drown
them in dressing or you'll lose the flavour. Borage tea can
be used to reduce fevers and as a systemic cleanser. Borage
should always be used fresh, not dried.

Celery and celeriac leaves
These contain many vitamins and minerals and dried
celery can be ground into a low-salt seasoning. Eating
celery is said to be very good for rheumatism as well as for
promoting restfulness and sleep.

Chamomile
It is important to distinguish between true chamomile
(*Matricaria chamomilla*) and other chamomiles. True
chamomile flowers should be carefully picked and dried
and then can be made into tea which aids digestion,
soothes and cleanses the whole digestive system and has an
antispasmodic effect. A very weak version of this can be
given to children from 3 months of age to ease diarrhoea.
Cold, the tea can be used on blonde hair to enhance colour

and shine and as a facial rinse to generally improve the skin. It is highly antiseptic and can be used to bathe wounds or in the bath. A poultice can be used to reduce abscesses and swellings, inflammatory pain, sprains and strains.

Chervil or sweet cicely

The root can be eaten or made into an infusion with water and brandy and used for coughs, flatulence and for general debility. This infusion is also said to be helpful for girls going through puberty, both to alleviate menstrual pain and to aid against outbreaks of acne. The leaves are often added to soups and sauces for their blood-cleansing properties. It also increases perspiration and has been used for fever, gout, skin problems and gallstones. Chopped and warmed leaves can be wrapped around bruises and painful joints.

Chives

This very mild form of onion has the reputation of stimulating the appetite and strengthening the digestive system. They are also known to improve the kidneys and lower blood pressure. Chives are an excellent addition to the diet of anyone recovering from a severe or lengthy illness.

Dandelion

This much maligned plant is actually an excellent addition to the medicinal garden, as it is full of vitamins and easy to grow! Young leaves can be torn and added to salads and sandwiches, or blanched and eaten as a vegetable. The roots can be dried, ground and made into a hot drink which is thought by some to be an improvement on coffee, having a stimulating effect without any side effects. It also aids the liver, kidneys and bowels to remain healthy and cleanse the system. Dandelion teas are used in the treatment of gallstones, liver disease and piles.

Dill

Dill seeds are infused to make a drink which aids digestion, cures stomachache, removes flatulence and promotes sleep. A weak version of this is often incorporated into gripe water for babies. Dill water will stimulate the appetite but chewing the seeds prevents hunger pains and removes bad breath. An astringent juice can be squeezed out of the whole plant and used as a dressing for piles and other swellings.

Elderberries and flowers

Both the berries and flowers make excellent wines, jams and jellies, and can be added to the cooking of meat, vegetable and sweet dishes. In addition, elderflower water makes an excellent facial rinse which cleanses and brightens, and if cotton pads soaked in it are placed over the eyes they will feel brighter and refreshed. Elderflower tea can be taken as a painkiller and is useful in the treatment of colds. Elderflower tea cleanses the blood and is slightly diuretic, so it can also speed recovery the morning after the night before! Elder leaves can be made into an infusion and rubbed onto the skin to deter flies and other insects. Elder leaves boiled until soft are useful for dressing bruises, strains, etc. However, I would not recommend using them on an open wound as, under some circumstances, they can be toxic.

Fennel

Fennel water is used to bathe the face, and soaked into cotton wool as a compress on the eyes, where it brightens and refreshes. Fennel seed tea is an excellent aid to the whole digestive system; removing any feelings of bloating or wind, curing flatulence, calming hiccups, nausea, vomiting and diarrhoea. It is also an excellent aid to those wishing to lose weight as it not only reduces the appetite but is said to actually promote weight loss. Fennel heads, the feathery tops, can be added to salads and are often added to fish dishes. The white bulbous root, often sold in shops as a vegetable, is Florence fennel and has a flavour similar to celery but sweeter with a faint aniseed taste.

Garlic

Garlic has long been recognized for its antiseptic properties. The juice, diluted with water, is added to dressings to prevent infection. Garlic is believed to cleanse the blood and stimulate the immune system. Added to hot water, or as an ingredient in soup, garlic is an excellent way of curing sore throats and alleviating the symptoms of colds. In my family we regularly take garlic and onion soup, or add them to casseroles, to prevent and treat colds in Winter. Bruised and mixed with lard, garlic used to be used as a Winter rub to prevent disease, alleviate asthma and treat whooping cough. Syrup of garlic also used to be given for the same problems. It is worth mentioning that if you cut garlic, rather than crush it, you will get more flavour and less odour on the breath or the skin. Grown amongst other plants it helps to deter pests.

Goldenrod (Solidago) An infusion of the leaves of goldenrod has a reputation for being excellent in the treatment of gallstones and other urinary problems. It is also of use in menstrual problems. The plant's older names of 'woundwort' and 'heathen wound herb', however, give a clear picture of its other uses. It is antiseptic, anti-inflammatory and will generally speed up healing. An infusion can be used both to cleanse and dress wounds and other injuries. As a spray it has also been used in cases of diphtheria. In powder form it can be used to treat old ulcers. Goldenrod is a favourite of many flower arrangers but be a little careful when handling it as the leaves and flowers contain a yellow dye which can stain.

Horseradish As well as having a very strong flavour, horseradish is a strong stimulant, both internally and externally. It promotes digestion and, because it contains antibacterial properties, is useful in cases of digestive upset. Scraped horseradish can be added to plasters and poultices and used to alleviate chilblains, neuralgia, sciatica, gout, rheumatism and other joint pains. Infused in milk or white vinegar it can be used to whiten the skin. Horseradish syrup can be used for coughs, bronchitis and hoarseness. It has also been used to expel worms.

Hyssop	Hyssop is known for its cleansing properties and is often added to food to help break down meat and reduce fattiness. As a tea it is used to reduce catarrh, relieve rheumatism and even asthma. An infusion of the leaves is often used to 'draw' bruises and reduce other discoloration of the skin. Fresh green leaves can be bruised and applied to cuts and scratches to speed healing. The green hyssop leaves are often added to liqueurs or cocktails.
Lemon balm (sweet balm, melissa)	Lemon balm infusion can be used to treat colds, flu and fevers. The tea has a calming and antispasmodic effect and is useful in treating morning sickness. If drunk regularly it will also increase mental powers and aid concentration, and is said to extend one's life span. It can also be used to cleanse sores and wounds, and if the leaves are added to a dressing it will help to keep a wound clean and infection free. Lemon balm is also a good plant for the garden as it attracts bees.
Lavender	Lavender is sometimes called the healing plant as its oil, whether applied or inhaled, is said to heal a wide range of problems. Use externally to heal all wounds, bruises, aches and pains. When inhaled it calms the mind, removes anxiety and depression, increases perception and brings about balance. However, the plant can also be used in a number of other ways. Lavender water, made by steeping crushed flowers in warm water and dabbed onto pulse points, calms, soothes, reduces headaches, anxiety and depression. It is used as a rinse to improve the skin and dark hair. Lavender tea made from the flowers is useful to calm and soothe the digestive tract, to cleanse the blood and to improve memory and sight. Dried lavender flowers are placed in sachets in drawers to scent clothes and keep moths at bay, under pillows to induce sleep and bring gentle dreams, and generally to scent the home. Lavender jelly makes an excellent condiment for most meats and fish.

Lavender stalks can be burnt on the fire or barbecue to scent the air and flavour the food, or they can be dried and used as incense sticks. Lavender soap not only cleanses, but helps to promote healing of the sort of scratches and marks that gardening leaves! If I could have only one plant it would be lavender.

Lovage

Lovage tea is gently cleansing, stimulates the digestive system and reduces flatulence. Although taken internally, the tea has a slight deodorant effect, reducing the effects of strong foods such as garlic, yeast and so on. Lovage leaves can also be added to the bath to produce the same effect. As I write, a friend of mine is testing lovage leaves under the insoles of her son's trainers – we await results! The leaves, when warmed in fat and placed on a boil or abscess, will quickly bring it to a head.

Marigold

Marigold flowers can be added to salads, where they brighten the appearance and add a slightly salty taste. The flowers can be soaked in oil or added to ointment and used to reduce the appearance of old and unsightly scars and skin eruptions, and make an excellent balm for tired feet. Fresh marigold flowers rubbed onto wasp or bee stings are said to reduce swelling and pain, and even to drive away warts.

Marjoram (sweet marjoram)

Marjoram is said to improve the circulation and the production of white blood cells, making it useful in fighting all kinds of infection. It can also be infused and used as a mouthwash, especially if there is any inflammation. Dried leaves and tops can be placed in a bag and warmed for use on sprains, bruises and aching joints.

Mints

There are a great many varieties of mint but all have similar uses, and choosing between them is mostly a matter of taste. For example, peppermint is generally hotter than spearmint. The best thing to do when choosing your plant is to pick a single leaf, crush it between your fingers and then both taste and smell it. You also need to bear in mind that small-leafed and low-growing mints will be less useful plants than their larger cousins, but all mints grow rapidly and are best confined in a container to prevent them taking over!

Mint teas are used to aid digestion, soothe digestive troubles, relieve stomachache and for their mentally stimulating properties. Mint can be added to a footbath to soothe sore and tired feet, or included in foot lotion. Mint leaves can also be chewed to ease toothache and to remove bad breath. It can be added to sleep sachets and pillows to promote rest and a good night's sleep. A sprig of mint worn when working or studying is said to increase mental powers. An infusion of mint can be used to rinse the hair to promote glossiness and to reduce dandruff.

Nasturtium

Nasturtium is a member of the watercress family and its leaves and flowers can be used in salads and sandwiches, where it gives a peppery flavour. Nasturtium contains a lot of vitamin C and has antibiotic qualities, and is thus useful in fighting off the onset of colds, sore throats, etc.

Nettle

Nettles are the bane of many gardeners' lives, which is a pity because they are mineral rich and have a number of uses. If you have enough space, try to section off an area for them, or keep them in a tub or barrel. Do not collect them from roadsides where they are contaminated by car exhaust fumes or from areas used by dog-walkers! Nettle tops can be added to soups and stews, or cooked in a similar way to spinach. Being iron-rich and containing many natural hormones, they are good for the blood and can be helpful during puberty. Fresh nettle juice can be used externally on a cloth, or taken internally to help stem bleeding. Placed on a compress it is thought to help dissipate rheumatic pains and the like. Nettle juice is also rubbed into the scalp to improve the condition of the hair and was thought to prevent hair loss.

Onion	Onion has similar properties to garlic (above) and, whilst you would need a fair-sized garden to grow enough for its culinary uses, it is worth growing a few plants for medicinal purposes if you can find space.
Parsley	Parsley contains vitamins A, B and C and is therefore a helpful addition to any diet. Chewed raw it will remove all trace of the strongest smell, even raw onion, from the breath, although do check you've no green pieces showing! Parsley is diuretic and helps to reduce excess water and bloated feelings before and during menstruation. It is an excellent aid to digestion when sprinkled on food and, as a tea, will help to reduce flatulence. Parsley tea has a reputation for helping reduce the inflammation of rheumatism. Parsley leaves can be placed over sore or inflamed eyes, and really do help the symptoms of hay fever. Historically, parsley was used to cure plagues, fevers, swellings and tumours.
Rose hips	Rose hips are the fruit of the wild dog rose and sweet briar rose. They contain high quantities of vitamin C as well as many other vitamins. Rose hip syrup is traditionally given to children as a vitamin syrup and can be added to foods to supplement the diet of those recovering from illness. Rose hip tea, as well as providing vitamins, is recommended as a diuretic and to assist in the function of the kidneys. Rose petals can be used to decorate salads and rose water (made by infusing them) is considered to be a safe eyewash and to enhance the skin. It is also recommended as a mouthwash and gargle. Given the amount of petals you need to make rose water, it's probably best to buy it at the chemist!
Rosemary	Rosemary is a stimulant, and particularly acts to increase the circulation and blood supply. In ancient Greece, students were encouraged to wear a garland or chaplet of rosemary to stimulate their mental powers; indeed, I rarely

work without a sprig close by! Rosemary tea is an excellent aid to digestion and is also helpful in moderating the appetite. It also removes headaches, lethargy and depression, and if taken in the early stages can help to reduce the symptoms of a cold. Applied externally it will aid healing by increasing the blood supply to the affected part. Rosemary water can be used as a hair rinse to promote shine, and is thought to stimulate hair growth and cure itchiness or dandruff. It can also be used in the bath or as a face wash to improve skin condition. Sprigs of rosemary can be placed on the barbecue to flavour food, or onto the fire to fill the room with a cleansing scent. Hung around the home, they are thought to be a barrier to disease and to deter flies.

Sage

Sage tea is a fine tonic and was considered to prolong life, increase wisdom and strengthen the memory. It is useful in dispelling colds and coughs, especially if also placed into a bowl of hot water and used as a steam bath. It is a disinfectant and makes an excellent mouthwash or gargle, and can be used to cleanse wounds. Sage tea was reputed to be useful in cases of typhoid, kidney and liver complaints, haemorrhage from the lungs or stomach, measles, pain in the joints, lethargy and a whole range of other ills including curing the bite of serpents! A strong infusion is said to darken the hair.

Sorrel

There are a number of sorrels, of which French sorrel has the most pleasant flavour. Sorrel is used to cool and cleanse the blood and to aid digestion, and is considered to help the kidneys and bowels. Sorrel root and seeds were traditionally employed to stop haemorrhage and bleeding. Sorrel tea is helpful whenever a cooling effect is needed, whether in colds and fevers or in stomach upsets. It has long been known in the countryside for its thirst-quenching properties, whether made into a drink or by chewing a single leaf. Sorrel leaves can be added to salads, or included in sauces where they will help to cut any fattiness in meat. Sorrel should not be eaten too frequently or by those who suffer from rheumatism due to its high levels of oxalic acid.

Summer savory

Summer savory, and to a lesser extent winter savory, has warming properties and is considered very useful in treating congestion. As a tea it can be given for coughs and other chest problems, and is believed to reduce lethargy. When the juice is mixed with a little oil it can be dropped into the ears to cleanse excess wax, and if added to a poultice is thought to be helpful for sciatica. A sprig of savory is very helpful if rubbed onto bee or wasp stings. Summer savory can be added to sausages, stuffings, pies or cooked with vegetables in the same way as mint. If cooked with beans it makes them easier to digest. It also makes an excellent garnish.

Thyme

There are a number of members of the thyme family, so it is possible to select the one which most suits your garden. It's worth noting that thyme, like mint, can take over if allowed to. Indeed, thyme lawns are often grown as a scented alternative, or addition, to grass. Thyme is rich in natural phenols and hence has long been used for its insect repellent properties. Sprigs can be placed amongst clothing to deter moths, or worn or carried in the pockets to keep away midges and the like. A sprinkling of fresh, crushed thyme on the windowsills helps to keep insects out of the house. The juice can be rubbed into the skin. Thyme has antiseptic properties and can be made into a wash and used to cleanse wounds and as a gargle, or the oil can be added to ointments and dressings. Chewing thyme leaves is believed to alleviate toothache. Thyme is also a deodorant and can be added to the bath, or eaten to counter strong food smells. Thyme has long been used in the treatment of eczema, psoriasis, ringworm and other skin complaints. In a steam bath thyme is very helpful for coughs and chest complaints and used to be recommended for whooping cough. A sprig of thyme placed under the pillow is said to enhance sleep and promote sweet dreams; certainly a bowl of dried thyme on the windowsill helps to sweeten the air of the sick room.

Vervain (verbena)   Vervain has long been considered a sacred herb, being associated with the Druids, Ancient Romans and Greeks. Although it has a bitter taste, vervain tea is recommended for headaches, stress, digestive troubles and as a sedative. It is also considered to have slightly aphrodisiac qualities. It can be used in poultices for aches including headache, although it will stain the skin a slightly reddish colour!

Woodruff   Woodruff tea has the effect of lifting the spirits and dispelling depression, and as such was often used at celebrations. Indeed the flowers and tops were often added to wine for Beltane celebrations, being both relaxing and uplifting. The flowers and young leaves were often strewn on the floor to give a pleasant scent to the home and to keep insects at bay.

Yarrow   Yarrow is felt to be effective in treating all digestive complaints and in regulating the blood. It is believed to be very effective for regularizing menstruation and reducing the oily skin of puberty, if taken regularly as a tea. Yarrow tea also helps alleviate severe colds and will help to break a fever by inducing sweat. It is felt to be useful in childhood illnesses where spots are involved as it promotes the outbreak and then the clearing of them. Yarrow poultices are felt to help staunch wounds and to reduce nosebleeds, although the ancients also recommended them to promote nosebleeds to relieve headaches! Yarrow leaves and flowers can be added sparingly, as it has a strong flavour, to salads, or included in sandwiches.

GATHERING YOUR PLANTS

As mentioned earlier, it is best to grow your own medicinal plants, for a number of reasons:

★ Assuming you have kept track of what is where in your garden and have taken care not to plant non-edible plants in the same area, you will know exactly what you are picking and avoid potentially dangerous mistakes.

★ Many of these plants are endangered or protected when growing in the wild. Just because you can see a lot in your neighbourhood does not mean that they are prolific.

★ Verges are subject to pollution from car exhaust fumes, parks and hedgerows are used by dog-walkers: either could result in some unwanted contaminants being present on, or in, your plants.

★ You can magically empower your plants whilst they are growing and reap the rewards when using them.

In most cases it is best to collect leafy plants first thing in the morning when the dew is still on them. Flowers and tops, however, prefer to be collected once the dew has dried. In most cases you will only want to take new growth, not old or woody bits. Use a sharp knife or scissors to cut your herbs, don't wrench them off by hand. Take care to check that the plant is healthy, and to deal with anything that it needs before you cut. However, if you feel that it needs water make sure that you do not water foliage or flowers whilst the sunlight is on them as they can be scalded, so either water at the roots or wait until sundown. Remember to thank the Elements, the Goddess and the God as you cut and to take only as much as you need. Place your cuttings onto a clean cloth, using a separate cloth for each variety, to bring into the house.

Once you have gathered what you need, rinse them gently under cold water and place on a clean cloth or absorbent paper to drain. Always use a sharp knife when cutting or chopping herbs, or for that matter anything in the kitchen. Having said that, many of the leafy herbs going into salads and the like prefer to be torn for use rather than cut.

DRYING AND STORING PLANTS

Whenever possible it is best to use fresh herbs, picked and taken straight into the kitchen, but a lot of these plants are seasonal, in which case you might like to consider drying them for later use. Plants intended for drying should be picked once the dew is off and placed in a single layer somewhere warm and dry. The flat net shapes designed for drying woollen jumpers are very useful if you have enough space to put them. As it can take anything from two days to two weeks to dry herbs, always ensure that you put out enough to let you test several samples. Some people have successfully dried herbs in the oven, but you will need a very low heat and absolutely no moisture in the air. Successfully dried herbs will be completely dry, almost crisp, and will have retained their colour. Any dried herb must retain its colour to retain its efficacy; faded or grey ones are ineffective. Even the best home-dried herbs tend only to keep for a few months so resist the temptation to cull whole bushes of them!

After you have dried your plants you will need to store them in airtight, moisture-proof jars, somewhere cool and dark. You can enhance their dryness by including a few grains of uncooked rice at the bottom of each jar. Label the jars carefully, including the name and date. You might also like to include information on the time of day you picked it, the phase of the Moon and so on. If you are storing plants for particular medicinal uses, you might like to keep them separate from your ordinary kitchen herbs to prevent them all vanishing into the cooking! Not only do home-dried herbs taste better than the ones from shops, but they also tend to have a stronger flavour.

MAGICALLY ENHANCING YOUR PLANTS AND RECIPES

Even when incorporating healing herbs and plants into everyday dishes or other applications, you can still use the Craft to enhance their powers.

Herbs and plants can be magically empowered or enhanced in different ways at different stages. When you plant them, you can ask for the Blessings of the Elements, the Goddess and the God in much the same way as you did when planting Living Spells as in Chapter 6. When you pick them you give thanks to the Elements, the Goddess and the God, as described above. When you actually prepare the tea or other remedy you can invoke the energies of the Goddess and the God, as follows:

Collect all your ingredients together. Before you actually start work, take a few deep breaths to centre and focus yourself. Invoke the Elements in turn saying:

'I call upon the Element of Air (Fire, Water, Earth) to lend your powers to this … (name of plant), that it might strengthen the healing of … (name of person).'

Take a moment to actually visualize Air (Fire, Water, Earth) and then say:

'Blessed Be.'

Now visualize the Goddess and the God and say:

'I call upon the Goddess and the God to empower this herb, that it might bring strength and healing to … (name of person). As you watch over the land and all living, watch over those in my care. Blessed Be.'

Now continue with your recipe whilst keeping in the back of your mind the thought of the person you are working for, the balance of the Elements you have invoked and the Goddess and the God. When you have finished, take a moment to thank the Elements, the Goddess and the God.

Remember you do not have to say any of these things aloud, you can do so just as effectively within your head.

PLANNING YOUR MEDICINAL GARDEN

Some people prefer to keep all their herbs and medicinal plants separate from the rest of the garden, for ease of identification, tending and gathering. Certainly, if you intend to grow edible herbs and poisonous plants in your garden it's a good idea to separate the two to avoid mistakes! If, like me, you have a tendency to forget what you have planted and where you put it, then it's a good idea to keep a label on or near your plants. Left over wooden lolly sticks are an inexpensive way of doing this, as are wooden chip forks, but make sure you write in indelible ink otherwise the first rainfall will undo your efforts!

A few plants really need to be confined, otherwise they can take over; mint and thyme are good examples of this. I find it's best to plant these in a large pot or other container and then to sink that into the soil. One friend of mine sinks old slate roofing tiles into the soil to partition rapid growers, although she still needs to be vigilant. Of course, if you have an area which you want filled, then this is ideal for these plants. The spreading properties of thyme and chamomile are sometimes exploited by creating a lawn with them. A lawn of herbs is wonderful to walk over as the scent will rise around you as you go. However, as it is not as hard-wearing as grass it really isn't suitable if you have children or dogs.

There are many ways of arranging medicinal plants, for example in alphabetic sequence, or by height. You could also order them by their effects; those good for limbs and joints together, those for digestive trouble, and those for the respiratory system. The only problem with this is that some plants have effects on several physical systems, although with enough space you could have one in each zone. In my garden my herbs are all planted so as to be accessible from the path and of those, the ones nearest to the house are the ones I use most often. Herbs, of course, can be incorporated into any of the planting schemes mentioned in previous chapters, and it can be beneficial to place them in amongst other plants as their strong scents help to deter bugs and pests.

One of the more interesting planting schemes I have seen was arranged along the lines of a spider's web. In this scheme the lines of the web were picked out using quite large pebbles, collected from the beach. Within the spaces various herbs were planted in alternating 'circle portions' of tall and short plants.

Another interesting idea I have seen involves creating an herb path. Here, a fairly wide crazy-paving path had a number of stones removed and low growing herbs were placed in the resulting gaps. This has the advantage of providing easy access to the herbs as well as isolating rapid growers.

An idea for those who are growing their herbs in the house is to paint each pot with the name of the herb as well as the ailments it is useful for. Alternatively, you could colour code their pots: yellow for respiratory helpers, green for digestives, etc.

BLESSING, DEDICATING AND CONSECRATING YOUR MEDICINAL GARDEN

When it comes to selecting which plants to grow in a Medicinal Garden it is usually better to buy them as you identify the need, rather than to go mad at the garden centre and end up with a wide range of things you will never use. As a result, it is more sensible to Bless and Consecrate each plant as you put it in, much in the same way as you magically empowered them above:

Take your plant, an appropriate digging tool and some water, to the spot you have selected for it. Take a few deep breaths to centre and focus yourself and then invoke the Elements in turn, saying:

'I call upon the Element of Air (Fire, Water, Earth) to lend your powers to this ... (name of plant), that it might strengthen its healing properties and bring health and strength to all who partake of it.'

Take a moment to actually visualize the Element and then say:

'Blessed Be.'

Now visualize the Goddess and the God and say:

'I call upon the Goddess and the God to empower this herb, that it might bring strength and healing to all who are given it. As you watch over the land and all living, watch over those in my care. Blessed Be.'

Plant your herb carefully in the ground, whilst thinking about the healing properties it contains. As you do so, say:

'In the Earth I place your roots that you may draw sustenance from it. In the Air your leaves and flowers reside that you may breathe. The light of the Sun shine on you to promote your growth. And as the gentle rain will fall on you, I water you to sustain your life.'

Water the plant in well, taking care not to splash the leaves and flowers if the Sun is hot. Then say:

'Blessed Be.'

Unless you are confident that you will remember what it is, label it clearly. When you have finished, take a moment to thank the Elements, the Goddess and the God.

CONTINUING CARE OF YOUR MEDICINAL GARDEN

In the early stages of an herb's life it is a good idea to regularly pinch out the tops to encourage new growth and a bushy habit. Indeed, many herbs will grow better if they are regularly picked. So make a point of visiting your plants regularly, at least once a week, to see how they are doing and to tend to them. Whilst you are checking your plants, it is a good idea to check their labels too. Many people set aside a regular day for this, chosen so that the following days are the most convenient for drying herbs. In a household where most people are out, at school or work on weekdays, Sunday would be a good choice, as the drying herbs do not then impinge on weekend activities. Many herbs are extremely sensitive to dry conditions, so if you have a hot, dry climate, or a spell of very hot weather, you might like to check on your herbs daily to see if they need water.

Whenever you tend your plants, or pick them for use, remember to give thanks to the Goddess and the God for supplying health and healing from the land.

EIGHT

THE SEASONAL GARDEN

As I mentioned in Chapter 1, in the Craft we have eight festivals called Sabbats, which taken together make up the Wheel of the Year, and these festivals are closely linked to the seasonal cycles and growth you can see in your garden and all around. Indeed, whilst the major festivals of Imbolg, Beltane, Lughnasadh and

Samhain have calendar dates set for them these days, many Witches will still celebrate them in the old way by waiting for the appropriate seasonal signs of snowdrops pushing through the ground, blossom on the hawthorn, the first harvest and the first Winter storms. The minor festivals of Yule, Oestara, Litha and Madron are the Solstices and Equinoxes which mark changes in the length of daylight and are hence determined by the passage of the Earth around the Sun. However, although the dates of these festivals are not determined by plant growth, they nevertheless have strong seasonal resonances.

In this chapter I am going to look at the garden from the perspective of the Wheel of the Year. We will see not only what happens in nature, but also how we can use our garden as both a seasonal indicator and for the celebration of our festivals. As one person put it, 'A garden is for life, not just for Summer.' The Wheel of the Year begins and ends at Samhain, and normally that would be the festival I would start with. Here, however, I will begin with Imbolg as this marks the start of the growing season. The dates alongside each Sabbat are those in common use amongst Witches and Pagans, but it is just as valid to work from the seasonal indicators alone. Seasonal indicators and garden projects will vary depending on where you live, but those below should give you guidelines from which you can plan your own year.

Traditionally, each Sabbat has a tree associated with it. If you can, find the appropriate tree for each Sabbat and make an offering to it. This could be a small loop of plaited grass, or a small piece of fruit placed in the soil at its base. Please ensure that whatever your offering, it is biodegradable and inconspicuous. If there is a piece of fallen wood nearby, take that home with you as a symbol of the Sabbat.

IMBOLG, 2 FEBRUARY

Imbolg literally means 'in the belly' and it is at this time that the first lambs are born. The first buds appear on the trees and we see snowdrops on our verges and in church-yards. Even where the ground is frozen and snow is upon the earth there are signs of the coming of Spring. This is a season where we can actually see the magic of nature in action. Try to make a point of visiting your local park and/or woods to see the changes taking place there, as well as observing those in your own garden. The tree associated with Imbolg is the ash.

This is the time to assess the garden and make good any damage caused during the Winter. If the weather is dry enough then attend to anything outside which needs painting before the new growth of Spring takes your attention and plants start to get between you and the chores! If your climate is fairly temperate, this is the time to sow seeds either indoors or in a greenhouse. Indoor plants should be checked over, and dusty foliage cleaned.

At Imbolg, the Goddess changes her robes of the Crone for those of the Maiden, and we celebrate her return by lighting white candles. At this time of the first indications of returning Spring it is a good idea to perform a blessing on the land and to invoke the energy of the Maiden to promote growth.

A BLESSING ON THE LAND

Make an asperger from a small bundle of twigs and take some sweet white wine or apple juice into the garden. Also take a white candle in a jar, or other windproof container. Make sure that you will be able to carry this safely back into the house, without burning your fingers, once it is lit.

Call upon the Elements in turn:

'I call upon the Element of Air (Fire, Water, Earth) to be present with me this festival of Imbolg. Pour your blessings on the land at this season of new growth. May new life spring from the land and may all be fruitful. Blessed Be.'

Visualize the Goddess as a beautiful Maiden, dressed all in white, with a circlet of fresh green shoots and white, star-like flowers. Visualize the God standing beside her as a virile young man, with all the promise of youth. Light the candle and say:

'I call upon the Goddess as Maiden, and the God full of youthful energy. Pour your blessings on the land. Bring new growth to plant, bird, fish and beast alike, bring new promise to this space and to all who share it.'

Hold up your glass of wine to them and say:

'Pour forth your blessings into this wine, that it may be a symbol of your love for the land and all who live upon it, and also a token of the care I commit myself to giving to all that lives and grows here. Blessed Be.'

When you feel that they have blessed the wine, take a small sip yourself and then walk the boundary of your garden. Using the asperger, sprinkle a little wine around all the edges. As you go visualize the Goddess and the God touching the plants and trees and new green shoots springing from everything they have touched. Remember to move deosil whilst doing this. When you have finished, thank the Elements, the Goddess and the God in the usual way and take the candle into the house with you. If you can do so safely, let it burn all the way down.

OESTARA, 21 MARCH

This is the Spring Equinox, when day and night are equal. From this point on, daylight hours become greater than those of darkness. Spring is now present, birds are building nests and seeking out their mates, many flowers like the crocus and daffodil are in bloom. If you have access to the countryside, look for hares boxing in the fields: the hare is sacred to the Goddess Eostar, a derivation of Astarte. Oestara's tree is the alder.

If you want to trim your hedges and bushes at the start of the season this is the time to do it, although personally I prefer to give them an Autumn cut, which carries less risk of disturbing early nesting birds. Plant out early seedlings and sow any remaining seeds. This is a good time to turn over your soil, remove any fledgling weeds and, if you have a lawn, prick it all over with a fork to aerate the soil. Take the time to check bushes, climbing plants and roses, to see if any need pruning. Take care not to remove all new growth. Give some thought to buying and planting some Summer fruiting plants, like wild strawberries. Plant garlic cloves in amongst your beds to help deter pests, and continue to be diligent with weeding. Plant sunflower seeds for a good display in Summer. If you have any major changes to make to your garden, this is the time to put them into action. Give all your houseplants an annual 'service'. Start children on their gardening projects to encourage an understanding of nature.

At this time of balance we seek to achieve balance in our lives and in all we do. It is a good time for sweeping away the old and bringing on the new.

TO PROMOTE NEW GROWTH

Before your Ritual think about the things in your life which are outworn and need replacing, such as bad habits, old guilt and so on. Think also of new ideas which you would like to take their place.

Take a new plant or seedling into the garden with you and find an old dead plant, or a dead part of a plant, already there. This should be something which has died naturally and not from disease. Call upon the Elements in turn saying:

'I call upon the Element of Air (Fire, Water, Earth) at this time of balance. Even as dark gives way to light, as day overtakes night, both are still necessary to the land. May all things be in balance to bring growth and fruitfulness to all living. Blessed Be.'

Visualize the Goddess, still as Maiden, but with flowers and leaves covering her dress and a hare at her feet. Visualize the God as a young man, accompanied by a young deer, and say:

'I call upon the Goddess and the God at this time of balance. Even as dark gives way to light, as day overtakes night, both are still necessary to the land. Sweep away the old that there be room for the new, let nothing that is outworn impede the growth of new life. Bring balance to all and growth and fruitfulness to the land. Blessed Be.'

Dig a suitable hole for your new plant. Then cut away the dead plant, or part of plant, and place a little of it in the bottom of the hole, saying:

'All things must wither and die, that new life may spring from them.'

Plant your new plant and say:

'From the old comes the new, from Winter comes Spring and from death comes life. May the Goddess and the God guide me in tending their land, may they lend their power to the growth of all. Blessed Be.'

Spend a few moments thinking about the things in your life that are outworn and visualize yourself burying these, and new ideas and aspirations growing from them. When you feel a sense of inner balance thank the Goddess and the God and the Elements and tidy away.

BELTANE, 1 MAY

Another name for the hawthorn is may, and Beltane has long been timed by the blossoming of this plant. This is the time of year when rapid growth takes place and many plants will come into flower. Two trees are associated with this festival, the hawthorn, or may, and the willow.

Plant out any remaining seedlings and start feeding all your plants. Unless the weather is really poor, this is the time to plant out anything which has been wintered indoors. Cut, or tie back, the greenery of daffodils, bluebells and the like, assuming they have finished flowering. If you have a pond this is the time to give it a check over and perhaps change most, if not all, of the water. Look to all your plants to see if any need thinning out, or if those with a bushy habit can be divided. Any fruits and vegetables really should be planted out now. Check your herbs – if you intend to keep and use them, it's a good idea not to let them flower. Start gathering and drying rose petals to make pot pourri, incense or for use in decorating containers.

At Beltane the Goddess sheds her robes of Maiden for those of the Mother, and the God takes his rightful place as her consort. Beltane marks their union for the fertility of the land. The maypole is a symbolic representation of this.

FERTILITY AND PROSPERITY OF THE LAND

In this Rite you will be making a scaled-down maypole. Depending on the size of your garden you can use anything from a whole broom handle to a small straight piece of wood about a foot long. To one end of this tie a number of brightly coloured ribbons, about three times the length of your wood. Make sure that you have at least one in bright red (for the Goddess) and one in bright green (for the God). If you have friends or family who like to join you in your Rites then have at least one ribbon for each person. Gather from your garden petals from a few flowers and/or some small sprigs of herbs.

'Plant' the broom handle or piece of wood into the ground, ribboned end uppermost, for about a quarter of its length. Call upon the Elements in turn saying:

'I call on Air (Fire, Water, Earth) to be present in this place. Bring fertility and prosperity to all the land and those who dwell on it. Blessed Be.'

Visualize and call upon the Goddess and the God:

'I call upon the Goddess and the God. Generous Mother and Father of all, whose union brings life and fertility to the land, be with me and with all who come to this place. Blessed Be.'

Now weave the ribbons around the pole, sending some around one way and others the reverse. Try to weave them in an attractive pattern which descends down the length of the pole to the ground. As you wind them, incorporate your petals and pieces of herb into the weave and chant over and over:

'Weaving in life, weaving in growth, weaving in fertility and abundance for all.'

When you reach the ends of the ribbons, tie them off around the pole, so that they remain secure. Uproot your finished maypole and, moving deosil, carry it around the outer edge of your garden. As you start out, say:

'The colours of the ribbons are the colours of the flowers, the wood is the growth of the trees. As the ribbons hold petals and herbs to the wood, may the Goddess and the God hold fertility to the land. Blessed Be.'

Go around the garden three times. If you have others with you, this can be made into a sort of relay dance with each person taking the maypole and dancing to the next until the pole has completed its three circuits. When you have finished, thank the Goddess and the God and the Elements. Place your maypole into the ground in the garden or into the soil of one of your pot plants to keep it in contact with the earth.

LITHA, 21 JUNE

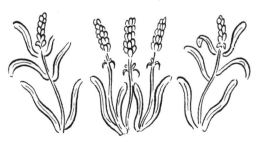

The Summer Solstice marks the height of the Sun; it is the longest day. From now on the days will shorten in length. This is the time when the Oak King gives way to the

Holly King. If you live in or near the countryside, you should see the crops ripening in the fields. Keep an eye out for the next generations of wildlife too. If you are likely to be driving in the countryside, please, please try to avoid slaughtering unwary rabbits, hares, ducks and other creatures. See if you can find a 'Pick Your Own' farm, and treat yourself and the family to a couple of hours tasting the best fruits. Oak is the tree of the Summer Solstice.

At this time you should be focusing on maintaining your garden by watering, feeding and dead-heading your plants. Ensure anything leggy has support and that climbers are actually headed where you want them. Be especially careful to ensure that plants in pots and containers are watered regularly, and not when the heat of the Sun is on them. This is the best time of year for taking cuttings if you want to propagate new plants from existing ones. Remember to take time to enjoy your garden!

Many people like to greet the Sun at sunrise on the Litha morning with chanting and drumming. However, do not, if you have neighbours, feel tempted to drum up the Sun in the early morning in your garden! If you really feel the Summer Solstice incomplete without drumming then take yourself off to an isolated hilltop, rather than rousing the neighbourhood and losing the goodwill of those you have woken. As it is at this time of year that we usually become aware of all the wee beasties who are eating our plants or interfering with their growth, I have focused here on a short Ritual to help drive them off.

REMOVAL OF PESTS

As I like to combine the practical with the magical you will first need to make your own insect repellent. Finely chop some onions and add them to a pint of cold water per onion. You will need enough to lightly sprinkle all your plants. Liquidize them and strain the resulting mixture. Put this into a plant spray or a watering can with a sprinkling 'rose'. This is not a recipe you will want to be using in the house, so if you only have indoor plants substitute a mixture of one pint cold water with two or three drops of washing up liquid, and place all your plants in the bath before you start.

Call upon the Elements:

'I call upon the Element of Air. Winds come and blow away all that might harm the growth in this garden. Blessed Be.
'I call upon the Element of Fire. Sun shine down and discourage all that might harm the growth in this garden. Blessed Be.
'I call upon the Element of Water. Rain fall and wash away all that might harm the growth in this garden. Blessed Be.
'I call upon the Element of Earth. Bring forth life that will consume all that might harm the growth in this garden. Blessed Be.'

Visualize and invoke the Goddess and the God:

'I call upon the Goddess and the God, protect the growth of this garden from all that might harm it. May your creatures which feast upon the plants find sustenance elsewhere, may your creatures which eat the enemies of plants find a haven here. Blessed Be.'

Take your insect repellent and say:

'Mighty Mother and Father of all, bless this water that it may drive away all that might harm the growth and fertility here. Blessed Be.'

Now, starting at the centre of your garden and moving deosil in a spiral, sprinkle all your plants very lightly, saying:

'Pests away, pests at bay, Lord and Lady drive the pests away.'

Try not to sprinkle yourself as the solution is quite pungent, and ensure that any pets are well out of the way, as onion water in the eyes will smart.

When you have finished, thank the Elements, the Goddess and the God and wash your watering can or spray thoroughly.

LUGHNASADH, 1 AUGUST

Lughnasadh is marked by the start of the harvest. These days a lot of farms are growing Maize Mazes. Not only are these great fun, but maze walking is a very old way of meditating on the land and bringing fruitfulness into your life. The Lughnasadh or Lammas tree is the hazel.

Continue general maintenance. Prune back anything which is threatening to take over, and give those roses which have finished flowering a really good trim. Many herbs can be propagated from cuttings at this time; I have found that placing them in a container of water which is full of pebbles or even marbles really seems to encourage rapid root growth. If your garden is looking good, take some photos to cheer you through the colder months. Visit your garden centre for end of season bargains.

Thus far all the Rites in this section have been primarily concerned with the growth in our own gardens, but it is fitting at Lughnasadh to work for the land as a whole. In the past the whole community would have turned out at this festival to take part in Rites intended to ensure a bountiful harvest.

A HARVEST OF PLENTY

If you can, obtain nine stalks of corn or barley with their heads intact – many florists sell them for dried flower arrangements. Make sure they are completely dry; you may need to place them in the warm for a couple of days to dry out. If you cannot get corn then look for grass with seed heads on it. Bunch eight of the stalks together and use the ninth to tie them in the middle. You will also need a sharp knife, a small amount of red wine or red grape juice, and either a pot and soil, or a small trowel with which to dig a hole. You will also need a fireproof container and some matches. As you will be burning a small amount of straw it really is best if you can do this outside.

Call upon the Elements in turn:

'I call upon the Element of Air (Fire, Water, Earth), be upon all the land, bring a harvest of plenty, that all might share and none go hungry. Blessed Be.'

Visualize the Goddess and the God holding the Earth as a small blue-green sphere between them and say:

'I call upon the Goddess and the God. Mighty Mother and Father of all life, bring a harvest of plenty to all the land, that none of your children need go hungry. Spread your blessings amongst all peoples and guide us, each and every one, to share in your blessings. Blessed Be.'

Now take your mini-sheaf of corn and cut off the heads whilst saying:

'This corn is but a token of the harvest we seek. As it bears the seeds of life, let life be upon the land.'

Put the heads to one side and place the stems in your fireproof dish and burn them, saying:

'As the stems burn they become ash which may fertilize the land to bring forth new life in the next season.'

Once they have burned, place the ash in the bottom of your hole or pot and cover with a thin layer of soil. Place the heads into the hole and sprinkle another thin layer of soil over them saying:

'We give to the earth that the land may know of our love and care for it, and that new life may grow.'

Sprinkle a little of the wine into the hole and say:

'This wine is as the life-blood of the land. As the life of the land is given up for us, so this wine is given up, to bring forth new life once more.'

Fill the hole in completely and pour any remaining wine onto the top. You might like to place a marker near the spot so that you know where to look for next year's growth.

Again visualize the Goddess and the God and say:

'Lord and Lady, know that we seek your blessing, not only for ourselves but for all your children. We thank you for your care and protection and ask that you continue to walk with us, each and every one, for all our days. Blessed Be.'

Lastly, thank the Elements in the usual way.

This Ritual is not going to bring an immediate stop to world hunger, but the more people who perform it, the more improvement we can hope to see.

MADRON, 21 SEPTEMBER

This is the time of the Autumn Equinox. Again, day and night are of equal length before the hours of darkness start to overtake the hours of light. The harvest is at its peak and this is a good time to seek out fruit and vegetable bargains which can be preserved or frozen for the Winter months. Apple trees are associated with this festival, especially crab apples. If you cut an apple in half across the core you will find at the centre a five-pointed star.

Cease feeding plants, but continue to water them if the weather is dry. Give some thought to bringing in any plants which are sensitive to frosts. Leggy plants should be checked to see that they are fully supported, before the Autumn winds arrive. Make a point of regularly clearing fallen leaves, or of digging them in between plants to nourish the soil. If, like me, you prefer to give bushes and hedges an Autumn trim this is the time to do it.

Madron, like Oestara, is a time of balance, but it is also the height of the harvest and it is a fitting time to give thanks for all we have been given. At this time our Rituals focus on whether we have paid for what we have received, not just in terms of tangible gifts but also of thanks for friendships, family and all the things we tend to take for granted in life.

GIVING THANKS FOR ALL THAT WE HAVE

In the period approaching this Ritual make a list of all the good things that have come to you in the past year: friends, family, health, the beauty of the earth, the cycles of the seasons and so on. Identify six reasonably large tasks which need attending to in your garden, and try to link them to the Elements, the Goddess and the God. For example:

Air	Trim hedges and high plants, ensure that climbers have supports to take them through the Winter.
Fire	Cut back any plants which are overshadowing others to let the light get through.
Water	Water all your plants, or attend to any tasks connected with a pond.
Earth	Dig fallen leaves into the soil, or turn over all the earth.
The Goddess	Create a wildlife refuge, it doesn't have to be large. A cluster of bamboo sticks cut into 6-inch (15-cm) lengths and tied together will become home to a variety of beetles. Of course if you have the space then consider a larger haven, perhaps to attract a hedgehog, or put up some boxes for birds or bats.
The God	Plant a berry-bearing bush for the birds. Berberis is a good choice as it comes in many sizes, or harvest sunflower seeds to feed them when the frost and snow come.

In this instance you will not be calling on the Elements, the Goddess and the God as you have done for previous Sabbats. You will, however, need to dedicate each task appropriately. Just before you commence each task, say:

'I dedicate this task to the Goddess (the God, the Element of Air, Fire, Water, Earth) as a token of my gratitude for all the blessings given to me this year. May my work bring a benefit to the land and be a fitting tribute to Her (Him, it). Blessed Be.'

As you perform each task, keep your purpose firmly in mind. If you have a lot of work to do, or cannot spare a lot of time all at once, work for each Element or deity on separate days.

SAMHAIN, 31 OCTOBER

Samhain is the most important festival in the Pagan and Wiccan calendar. It marks the end and beginning of the year. It is the beginning of the resting season for the land and at this time we see many things dying back. The first frosts will be coming and the first storms of Winter will be upon us. Even if it is cold and wet, try to make a point of once again walking in the woods to see the changes taking place. Samhain's tree is the elder, which should never be burnt.

Plants in pots and containers need to be protected from the cold of Winter. If you cannot bring them in, wrap several layers of newspaper or straw around the pots to help keep the frosts off their roots. Put an inflatable ball or empty plastic bottle in your pond to help counteract freezing water. Visit any nearby woodland to see if you can find two or three fallen branches, or pieces thereof, to make a small woodpile home for beetles, etc. If you are considering a bonfire at this time of year, remember to stack the wood in one place and only move it to the fire site at the last minute. This way you are less likely to cook hedgehogs! Start to feed the birds. Make a point of checking the children's garden area if you have one. Clean, oil and generally service all your gardening tools and put them away securely.

At Samhain, the Goddess changes her robes of Mother for those of Crone, and the God rides out on the Wild Hunt to gather up the souls of those who have moved on from this life. It marks the start of the resting season for the land and a more contemplative period for the people. Samhain is also a time of divination and of scrying. There are many ways of seeking to find out what is in store for us, many of which are traditional to this time of year. A lot of these are linked to love and romance. For example, a woman with two suitors will take two acorns and name each after one of them. She then places these in the fire and the one which bursts first will be the man she will marry. The peel of an apple, removed in one piece, is thrown over the shoulder to indicate the initial of a future spouse. However, as our lives are more complicated than just identifying a partner, here we will try a more flexible technique.

SEEKING TO KNOW THE FUTURE

This technique will allow you to ask several questions, although you will need to form your questions so that the answer will be 'yes' or 'no'. Before your Rite, find several jars of roughly equal size – you will need one for each question you would like to ask, plus an extra 'timing' one. You will also need a tea-light candle per jar and a spill or taper so that you can light the candles without burning your fingers. Write your questions on slips of paper which can be placed under the jars to identify which is which, and you may find it useful to have a separate paper and pencil to note down the results.

At dusk on Samhain eve take your jars, candles, etc, outside. This form of divination will not work indoors. Place a candle into each jar and arrange them in a fairly tight circle, which you will be able to walk around.

Call upon the Elements:

'I call upon the Element of Air (Fire, Water, Earth), be with me and guide me this Samhain eve. Blessed Be.'

Visualize the Goddess as Crone, dressed in black with a veil over her head, and the God as a Huntsman about to ride out, and say:

'I call upon the Old Gods – upon the Goddess as Crone, bringer of wisdom, and the God as leader of the Wild Hunt. At this time of Samhain, when the veil between the worlds is thin, guide me to knowledge and understanding. Blessed Be.'

Read through your questions and place a question paper under each jar. If you are not sure whether you should ask a question this is the time to abandon it. You should have one jar with no question, which you will use to set a time for the answers to be determined.

Light all the candles, using the taper, starting with the timing candle first. Walk deosil around the outside of your circle of candles, watching them carefully, until the timing candle goes out. Candles which go out before the timing candle have 'yes' for an answer, those which are still alight when the timing candle goes out have 'no' for an answer. The candles will go out in the same order as the events will happen, i.e. first out will happen first, and so on. If the night is very windy you will have to watch very carefully to determine the order in which they go out. If the night is very still, increase the pace at which you circle the group. Note down your results and then thank the Elements, the Goddess and the God as usual.

YULE, 21 DECEMBER

The Winter Solstice marks the longest night, and from here the hours of daylight increase once more. Even though the coldest days are still to come we can look for the first snowfall and the tracks of wild animals in the snow. At this time the Holly King once more gives way to the Oak King. Bring evergreens into the house to celebrate the fact that, even in the depths of Winter, there is still life. The tree of the Winter Solstice is the Holly. If you wish to pick Holly to bring into the house make sure that you leave an offering of honey and raisins. Mistletoe is also a seasonal plant for this time, but unless it is very prolific in your area do not take it from the wild. Even if it is abundant only cut a small part of any one plant as it is becoming harder to find each year. Remember to save the berries to put out for the birds so they may play their part in its life cycle for next year's plants.

Focus on protecting plants from wind, cold, frosts and excess water. If you use weedkiller on paths, etc, this is the time to put it down. Personally I prefer manual weeding as it is less likely to kill off wildlife. Make a point of breaking the ice on your pond to allow the water to oxygenate. Ensure that you continue to feed the birds, by making or buying fat balls for them. If local ponds are frozen, also put out water for the birds daily.

Yule is the time when we celebrate the return of the Sun, as the decreasing day length gives way to increasing light. It is also a traditional time to celebrate with friends and family.

AFFIRMING BONDS OF FRIENDSHIP AND FAMILY LIFE

Make a list of your near and dear, friends and family. This shouldn't be too arduous as you probably made a Christmas card list earlier in the month! Remember to include anyone with whom you would like to renew contact. Purchase some sweet pea seeds, enough for one more person than you have on your list. You will also need some seed compost and a seed tray, or a selection of pots to sow the seeds in. Prepare the seed tray, pots and compost to receive the seeds prior to starting your Ritual.

Call upon the Elements in turn:

'I call upon the Element of Air (Fire, Water, Earth) at this festival of Yule. Be with me and lend your aid to strengthen all ties with those I love and hold dear. Blessed Be.'

Visualize the Goddess and the God:

'I call upon the Goddess and the God, the Moon and the Sun together. Wherever your light falls may it light up the lives of those I love and hold dear, may it strengthen our ties and bring us closer together. Blessed Be.'

Now plant your seeds, one by one. As each goes into the soil name a person from your list. The last seed will not have a name but should be planted for *'the friends yet to come'*. Lightly water the seed tray, cover it with cling film and place it somewhere warm with a temperature which does not fluctuate too much. Thank the Elements, the Goddess and the God in the usual way. When your seedlings sprout you can remove the cling film. If they develop flowers when still small pinch these out as soon as they appear. If your crop does really well, you can always give the young plants to friends and family.

Once you have completed a full cycle of the Wheel of the Year through your garden you will have gained a far greater understanding of the seasons, the festivals and the way in which they relate to the growth of plants and life. You may also find that your enhanced perspective gives an insight into the way other living things fit into the life of the earth. To make the most of your experiences and insights it is well worth keeping a journal throughout the year. Make notes on how your plants are faring, the tasks you do in your garden, the wildlife which passes through, the festivals you celebrate and the magics you work. All this will help you build up a picture of your own piece of nature and will help you to garden more effectively in future years.

NINE

TINY AND INDOOR GARDENS

Although I've mentioned small gardens throughout the rest of the book I feel that they, and the problems they pose, deserve a chapter of their own. Not everyone is blessed with a large outdoor area, or one which they can make changes to. I can appreciate the problems of the small, or even non-existent, garden because I too have lived in a flat with no garden, and a house with a piece of 4 x 10 foot (1 x 3 m) concrete, most of which never received any light. But neither of these has stopped me from growing at least some plants or from incorporating nature into my Rites and Rituals. Your outdoor space may be a balcony, your windowsills or nothing at all. In this chapter I hope to give you some ideas which you can use to bring a bit more life and nature into your home.

One of the keys to making a small garden seem larger is to create the illusion of space. Objects peeking through the foliage give the impression that there is somewhere behind and an even greater illusion of depth can be gained using mirrors. Because they reflect light and the backs of plants, mirrors can appear to be a window onto another area. Another technique which helps to fool the eye into believing that there is more space is to avoid straight lines and obvious corners. A curved or winding path will give a greater illusion of space than a straight one. A single plant placed slightly away from an edge fools the mind into thinking there must be more space behind it. If corners can be rounded, perhaps with a curved display of pots, then the mind loses the angle and pushes the edges back. It's also worth noting that if you place a biggish plant outside a window then the room that looks onto it will also seem larger too. If you have enough space, a strategically placed door, either real or painted, implies that there is another space beyond the boundary.

However small the width or length of your outdoor area, there is one dimension which is not restricted: height (so long as you do not block your neighbour's light, that is). With a little imagination a wide variety of objects can be utilized to create a garden which is more vertical than horizontal.

THE VERTICAL GARDEN

Although I have recently moved to a house with a good-sized garden, last year saw me with the above-mentioned rectangle of gloomy concrete. Not only that but it also had to be the 'garden' for both my son and my dog, and seemed to be infested with snails which ate everything in sight! As you can imagine, it was hard to grow anything there, but with a bit of improvisation I managed a quite passable effort. Using planks of wood on beer barrels I managed to elevate all my pots so that they received enough light, and were kept out of doggy reach. The purchase of a jasmine and a climbing rose helped me to partly cover the brick wall my window looked out over, and with a carefully placed Green Man peeking through their foliage I managed at least the illusion of depth. With window boxes firmly attached to the windowsills I had my herbs lined up outside the kitchen window, and could then see enough green to remind me that life was indeed present.

You may not need to raise all your plants quite so high but even raising a few at the back of a patch will make the area appear larger. If you can organize them into layers then you will gain real additional growing room as well as hiding unsightly walls or boring fences.

PLANNING YOUR VERTICAL GARDEN

The most obvious way of extending your garden is to use the windowsills. Indeed window boxes are, for some, the only garden they have. Carefully planned, a window box can be used to grow a wide variety of plants – I know of at least one person who has grown vegetables in theirs. The important thing is to ensure that your window box is securely fixed to the windowsill, especially if you are on the first, or higher, floor. A falling pot plant or whole window box is extremely serious if someone happens to be passing beneath it! Even if your windowsill itself is narrow you can get sturdy brackets which will attach the box to the wall. The other consideration with window boxes lies in watering. Please make sure that any excess does not water passers-by or pour into a downstairs neighbour's window! Window boxes are really excellent for herbs as you can keep them in their pots and place the pots in the box, avoiding any concerns about rapid growers taking over. Otherwise, when choosing plants, try to avoid anything that is likely to grow too quickly, or has a likely height more than twice the depth of the box – a good rule of thumb for determining how much soil it is likely to need.

One of the best ideas I have come across for vertical planting is the use of a stepladder. Steps sloping up a wall will give you several surfaces on which to place your pots and the sides can be used to train climbing plants. Old-fashioned wooden steps are the most attractive, and can sometimes be bought second hand, but even a metal

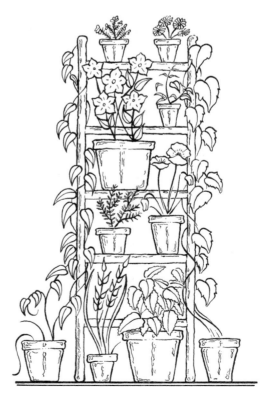

stepladder will house a large number of pots. Each step will take two to three pots and if you alternate upward-growing plants with trailing ones you will soon have a garden which hides the bulk of the ladder. It's important to ensure that your pots will not fall off the ladder, or any other high place, and for this I find that a re-useable adhesive gum, like Blu-Tack, is an excellent way of attaching them. Be careful to ensure any ladder does not provide burglars with easy access though!

An extension of the stepladder idea is to buy three or four planks of wood of decreasing width, and get hold of some house bricks. You can then build your own 'steps' by placing a couple of bricks at intervals and placing the widest plank on them. For the next step place three bricks on the wide plank, immediately above the first bricks and place the second widest plank on them. Continue until you have your steps completed. You will only be able to use the front edge of each of the lower steps for plants, as the backs will be in darkness, but they can be used for empty pots, tools, etc.

All manner of discarded items, including furniture, can be used to build a raised corner. Start at the back with the highest piece and place lower pieces around it until the second to front row is made of inverted plant pots, and the front row is plants in pots on the ground. Again, the use of climbers at the back and trailing plants within the design will give maximum cover of the items you are placing your plants on. And if you are not keen on fixing a trellis, wire or mesh to a wall you can always train your climbing plants using a cheap clothes horse!

Second-hand shops are a veritable mine of useful bits and pieces, if you are prepared to use your imagination. If you have a wall which receives good light then attaching an old bookcase to it will give you several shelves on which to put pots, and if high enough, all should receive good light. Old bowls, pots, pails, urns and so on make attractive planters, and can always be painted if they are too scruffy. I have heard of people who use discarded car tyres stacked up to create vessels deep enough for potatoes and, more attractively, a strawberry tub. I even have one friend who has planted up a bathtub and a couple of discarded toilets!

Even in a tiny garden you can still have a mini-pond or even a fountain if you choose something small enough. It might be best not to try to incorporate fish as the water in a small container may freeze solid in Winter or become too warm in Summer. Having said that, there are a number of plants, including dwarf waterlilies, which can be grown if you can get the depth right. A small water feature will need careful attention to ensure that it does not get too much heat, cold or even become clogged up with algae, but it does make a pleasant addition to the small garden. And the sound of even the smallest fountain again helps to create the illusion of space.

When you have very little room it's tempting to concentrate on plants alone, but a little ornamentation will fool the mind into thinking there is more space than there is. Of course, just because something is ornamental does not mean it cannot be functional! So look for decorated planters or plaques which are attractive as well as holding a small plant.

USING YOUR VERTICAL GARDEN

The size of garden we are discussing here makes it unlikely that you will be able to work much in the way of group Ritual in it. However, as long as there is enough room for you to stand, sit or kneel, there is no reason why you should not be able to work on your own. Solitary Witches do not need to wave their arms around, nor do they need to speak aloud. If you have selected plants as Elemental markers you can take them from their regular site for your working and replace them after, or you can take your plants indoors for workings and celebrations. But the main objectives in creating a garden are, firstly, to give you access to nature and secondly, to allow you the opportunity to work with the land and growing things.

A SPELL FOR SECURITY AND PRIVACY

If you have a tiny garden it is more than likely that you are living in a high-density area, and privacy will be at a premium. Whilst this spell will not make your neighbours further away, it will have the effect of making them less interested in you and what you are doing. Collect some rain, sea or river water, and some salt. Take both into your Vertical Garden one evening during the Waning Moon, at least three days after the Full Moon.

Call upon each of the Elements in turn:

'I call on Air to be with me here. May the thoughts of those around turn from this place and keep its secrets. Blessed Be.

'I call on Fire to be with me here. May the gaze of those around turn from this place and find other places more interesting. Blessed Be.

'I call on Water to be with me here. May those around find interest in their own lives and not mine. Blessed Be.

'I call on Earth to be with me here. As the boundaries are marked may none stray over them without invitation. Blessed Be.'

Then invite the Goddess and the God:

'I call upon the Old Gods. May the Goddess and the God watch over this place and all who dwell in it. May they guard, guide and protect us in all we do. Blessed Be.'

Take your salt and, walking deosil around your outdoor space, sprinkle a little on the ground saying:

'I cast a Circle round about, with salt to keep all evils out.'

Then take the water and sprinkle that deosil around your space:

'Cast the Circle once again, with water as the falling rain.'

Finally walk the area deosil, touching your boundaries as you go:

'Spirit hold the Circle fast, a mighty wall, built to last. Blessed Be.'

Pause for a moment and visualize a great barrier rising up around you on all sides, which will protect your home, family and garden. When you can see it clearly, then you should thank the Old Gods and the Elements.

Many people like to extend this spell to include their whole home and garden. In this case you will need to plan a route which takes you through the whole ground floor of your house, deosil. Take care when sprinkling salt and water indoors that you go behind all pieces of furniture and do not sprinkle electrical equipment!

THE INDOOR GARDEN

When I was young we lived in a flat with some really quite strangely shaped rooms, caused by it being the conversion of an old house. One of these 'rooms' was in fact a corridor, which at one end was nearly 8 feet (2.5 m) across. And although we did have a garden, my Mother termed this corridor-room 'The Garden Room'. With the addition of some old second-hand furniture this room became home to a huge variety of plants, and also the nursery for seedlings intended to go out later. In fact, she became so fond of having a Garden Room that in subsequent homes there was always a room, or part room, which became an indoor garden. But even if you do not have enough space to set aside a whole area you can still use windowsills, or the area just in front of a window, as a growing space. If you have several windows which can be used, then your plants can also be scattered around the house. Forget the old wives' tale about plants in the bedroom being bad for your health – yes, they give off CO_2 at night, but very little, and besides you do not sleep in a hermetically sealed box! You may find that some plants are too highly perfumed to keep in the bedroom, but that is a question of personal taste. I would also refrain from placing anything poisonous in a place which is accessible to children or pets, just to be on the safe side.

PLANNING YOUR INDOOR GARDEN

There is virtually no limit on what can be grown indoors, so long as you take into account the three main constraints of light, water and, most importantly, how much weight your floor can take!

Light

Light and warmth are essential to plant growth. However, plants indoors can be more susceptible to excess sunlight than those outside. South-facing windows (north if you live in the southern hemisphere) are often too well lit in the

Summer. Plants in strong direct sunlight dry out very quickly and can easily scorch, especially if the light is coming through glass. Some plants will thrive under these conditions but most prefer indirect light, or direct light when the Sun is well past its zenith. If you are in doubt as to a particular plant's preference, then check on it morning and evening for at least a week to see how it is faring. North-facing windows (or south in the southern hemisphere) suffer from the reverse problem, in that they often do not get enough light to enable plants to grow well. You can always supplement the light a plant receives by using a lamp with a special daylight bulb, but it can be far more attractive to position a mirror, or mirrors, behind your plants to increase their light and make it look as though you have a positive rainforest! Carefully positioned, mirrors can also be used on the lower portion of south-facing windows to enable you to screen excess light whilst not ruining the view.

Water

Water is also essential to plant growth, however it is not so good for carpets, wallpaper and wooden furniture. Individual plants can be placed on saucers, special potholders or any other water-retaining object. Not only will these protect your home; they allow you to water the plant from the bottom and to leave a little extra for thirsty plants. If you are setting aside a biggish area, then consider putting a waterproof liner under that space. A liner can be made from a bin bag, but there are more attractive options. Consider buying a small piece of attractive but waterproof floor covering, plastic tablecloth or picnic sheet. You will still need to place individual pots in holders, but the liner will prevent damage done by spills or accidental over-watering.

Weight

If you really wanted to you could grow potatoes indoors! However, you do need to consider whether your floor will take the weight. Even the ground floor of some houses will have a space underneath and too heavy a container will eventually bend and possibly break the floorboards. Remember, too, that a well-watered plant will weigh considerably more than a dry one and, Goddess willing, that your plant will get bigger. A plant in a pot full of damp earth may not weigh as much as you, but you are not a 'dead' weight, nor will you be stood in the same place for months on end. If you propose to line your plants up in a row, it is also worth checking that it's not just the one floorboard which will be taking the weight. Similarly, if placing plants on a piece of furniture, give some thought as to whether its weight is evenly distributed or whether the four legs or wheels are going to punch four holes in the floor! In both the latter cases you might want to place a board under your waterproof liner to spread the weight.

One idea for an indoor garden is to set aside one corner of a room as your garden area. Place a waterproof liner on the floor, preferably with an undulating edge at the front. Put mirrors against both walls, or across the corner, to reflect light and increase the apparent depth of the area. At the back place plants on top of inverted pots and perhaps one or two climbers, which can be trained using bamboo poles or hoops. Graduate the height of plants down to the front edge. As that edge is curvy some plants will stick out further into the room than others, again increasing the illusion that there is more to the area than there really is.

If you have wide internal windowsills, these are excellent for putting your plants on but most modern homes have small or no windowsills, so you might like to place a table or bookcase in front of the window to gain the same effect. To utilize the vertical element, a bookcase with its back removed can be placed on top of this, so long as you still get enough daylight.

It can be interesting, when planning an indoor garden, to choose the plants which match or complement your existing colour scheme. Alternatively, pick just two or three colours to base your garden on – having plants with, say, a purple and blue hue will give a feeling of tranquillity. A scheme based on red, orange and yellow will be energizing and cheerful. Try not to overdo it with heavily scented plants, as on warm days you will be overpowered with the combined perfume.

The kitchen windowsill has long been a favourite place for herbs, and is of course ideally suited for those which you will be using in cookery or for medicinal purposes. But I would like to take this opportunity to remind you that plants placed too near the cooker, washing machine, sink, etc, will suffer from the heat and steam generated. The same thing applies to plants in the bathroom. Also, plants over the sink should be far enough away that they do not get splashed with washing-up water – detergent does not taste nice in the subsequent use of them!

If you are really short of space then you can always plant a mini-garden in a large pot, bowl or tub. A preserving pan or even an old fashioned stove top boiling pan can be pressed into use and several plants grown in it. If you choose small, slow-growing plants then you should be able to get quite a few into a relatively small vessel. Of course, you can always use a bottle garden or a herbarium to the same effect. A fish tank can also be converted into a garden, although as it is watertight you will need to be very careful not to over-water.

When creating a garden in a small space it is easy to think only of the plants, but the addition of one or two attractive stones and perhaps a statue or two can really help to bring it to life. The contrast between living and inanimate objects can make a collection of plants appear far more than it actually is. Furthermore, basing your display around a statue of your favourite deity makes your indoor garden a shrine to them. Pebbles scattered between your pots can also disguise your waterproof liner and give the whole area a more outdoors feel. Candles, too, can be placed in amongst your plants, so long as you are certain they are safe and will not burn the foliage.

USING YOUR INDOOR GARDEN

Just as with the Vertical Garden, you can always move your plants whenever you need to, but you might find that it is possible to choose plants which can remain in the quarters all the time. Of course, the real advantage of an indoor garden is that you are not going to be overlooked by curious neighbours, so your uses are not going to be limited to what may feel unnoticed.

A SPELL TO FIND THE RIGHT PLANT

Sometimes it can be really hard to find exactly the right plant for your needs. I know I find it irritating to have researched and selected just the right one, only to find nowhere seems to have it in stock. At these times I use the following spell.

This Rite is best performed at, or just after, the New Moon. Either find a picture of your chosen plant or sketch one onto a small sheet of paper. If you aren't certain exactly what plant you want, then list the attributes you want it to have: size, colour, scent or no scent and so on. If you have plants with similar attributes, say one with the right size of leaf, or another with the right colour flower, then take one leaf from each of those. You will need a fireproof dish and a heat-resistant mat to stand it on, a self-igniting charcoal block, some incense or, even better, a sprig of rosemary, and some matches. You will also need a small amount of water and a pot with a little soil in it.

Call upon the Elements, visualizing each in turn:

'I call upon the Element of Air to be with me. May the gentle winds bring the knowledge I seek. Blessed Be.

'I call upon the Element of Fire to be with me. May the light of the Sun inspire me. Blessed Be.

'I call upon the Element of Water to be with me. May the lifeblood of the land guide me. Blessed Be.

'I call upon the Element of Earth to be with me. May I find that which I seek to plant in its embrace. Blessed Be.'

Now visualize the Goddess and the God. If there is one particularly associated with your plant, focus on that Deity.

'I call upon the Goddess and the God. Guide me in my search for … (name of plant, or recite the attributes from your paper). Show me the places to look and the way to care for it, even as you care for all living. Blessed Be.'

Next, light your charcoal and place it in the heatproof dish. When you are sure that it is burning, sprinkle your incense or rosemary on to it. Take your picture, or list of the plant's attributes, light it and place it on top of the incense. Watch it as it burns and say:

'As smoke rises take my message to the winds. As Fire burns bring inspiration. As the Earth to which all returns is here show me the way. As Water flows, guide my steps.'

Once the paper has completely burned away, sprinkle a few drops of water onto the charcoal block. Try to ensure it has gone out, but do not flood the dish. While you are waiting for it to cool enough to handle, meditate and visualize yourself finding and buying the plant. Once the charcoal and ashes have cooled, bury them in the pot, and put it to one side until you find your chosen plant, when the contents can be disposed of.

Complete your Ritual by thanking the Goddess and the God, and the Elements. Also make a point of tending all your existing plants at this time whilst keeping in mind the new addition you are seeking.

CONTAINERS FOR PLANTS

Plant pots do not have to be boring! Whilst it is best if a plant's immediate home has drainage holes, the vessel you place that into can be anything which is watertight. Next time you are shopping look around at all the different things which could be used to hold plants, or even open your cupboards and give some thought to what you already have. Souvenir mugs and cups can house small plants, and any kind of dish or bowl can be pressed into use; it can be a good way of giving new life to chipped or lightly cracked favourites. I have even seen an impressive indoor garden planted in chamber pots.

Not only can you look for attractive containers but you can also decorate pots and other vessels. Children's paint mixed with PVA glue is cheap, effective and will survive the occasional splash of water. Not only that, but if you have children it makes a good rainy day activity. Try finger painting flowers and leaves. PVA glue can also be used to stick things onto pots. I recently saw an old plastic fast-food container which had been covered in glue and then rolled in dried lavender, giving it a really interesting texture as well as a scent of its own. Other dried herbs could also be used in this way – it's a good way to use up out of date ones! Alternatively, you could stick feathers, shells, dried flowers, small pebbles or even gemstones onto your containers. Pictures can be glued on and then sealed with a coat of PVA mixed with an equal amount of water. This can look especially effective on glass or transparent plastic containers.

CONTINUING CARE OF YOUR POT PLANTS

Plants in pots are totally reliant on you to care for them, to ensure that they have the right kind of light and enough, but not too much, water. It's best to check them once or twice a week. Over the years I have found that one of the best ways of reminding myself to do this is to keep a particularly thirsty plant in a prominent position. As soon as this starts to look a little limp, I'm reminded to check all the others! My current thirsty friend is a potted buddleia which droops quite dramatically the moment its soil gets less than wet! Not all plants will require the same amount of water, or watering at the same time. Until you get to know each plant's preference, the easiest way to check is to touch the soil with your fingertip. If it's dry, water the plant, otherwise leave it until next time. I also treat my pot plants to a good soaking once or twice a year. Place all your pots into the sink or bath and slowly fill with cold water up to about half an inch below the level of the top of the smallest pot. If you have a wide range of pot sizes you might like to do small ones first and then the larger ones in a deeper bath. Leave them to soak for an hour and then drain them for a further half hour, before putting them back into their containers. Pot plants also appreciate the occasional shower, which can be achieved either by standing them outside in the rain, under a watering can with a sprinkler attachment, or under a gentle cold shower in the bathroom.

From time to time pot plants need feeding, usually more in the Spring and Summer than in the Winter. Buy a proprietary plant food and follow the instructions on the packet. Don't be tempted to overfeed, more is not better.

Also check the bottom of the pots regularly, if roots are beginning to show then it's time to think about the next pot size up. Generally speaking, it is not a good idea to pot on something which is about to flower as it often causes the plant to put all its efforts into new root growth to the detriment of blooms.

For plants in pots I do not use full-size garden tools, but have a dessertspoon, kitchen fork and a small pair of household scissors reserved for indoor gardening.

A SPECIAL RITUAL FOR YOUR POT PLANTS

If your plants are to form a part of your Craft in any way, then you will be including them in your Rituals. But it is also a good idea, once or twice a year, to hold a Ritual especially for your plants. I like to do this at the Spring Equinox when the growing season is well under way, but you can select the time of year which seems most appropriate to you.

In the week before my Ritual I prepare by checking over all the plants. Firstly, I select one which I will not tend to just yet. The others have a full 'service': I pot on any which have grown too big for their pots, trim off any dead leaves, cut back any which are too leggy, remove any dust from their leaves, clean the pots and containers, and maybe even redecorate any which need it. The one plant not included at this time is reserved for attention in the Ritual.

For the Ritual you will need the plant which has been set aside, a new pot and soil if it needs potting on, a damp cloth to clean its pot and a dry one to dry it, a new container and any other bits and pieces required to bring it back to peak condition. You will also need enough water to water-in that plant and to give each of your others a small amount.

Firstly visualize and call upon the Elements in turn:

'I call upon the Element of Air, which is needed that all living things may breathe. Be with me now and with all I care for. Blessed Be.

'I call upon the Element of Fire, which is needed that all living things may have warmth and light. Be with me now and with all I care for. Blessed Be.

'I call upon the Element of Water, which is needed that all living things may drink. Be with me now and with all I care for. Blessed Be.

'I call upon the Element of Earth, which is needed that all living things may have sustenance. Be with me now and with all I care for. Blessed Be.'

Then visualize the Goddess and the God:

'Gracious Goddess, Mighty God, Mother and Father of all life and all living, be with me now and with all I care for. Blessed Be.'

Now take your plant and the equipment needed to tend it. Trim and tidy it, re-pot it if necessary, clean its pot and container and, if it is dusty, give the leaves a gentle wipe over. Whilst you are doing so, think about all your plants, and also take the time to look outside at any other growing things you can see. In your mind visualize the Goddess and the God walking across the land, tending and caring for all living things. When you have finished tending your plant, take the water and, holding it in both hands, say:

'I call upon the Goddess and the God to bless this water, may it nourish and sustain this and all my plants, as it nourishes and sustains all life.'

Visualize the Goddess and the God pouring their energy into the water as a stream of gold and silver particles. When you feel that they have done so, say:

'Blessed Be.'

Now water-in your plant, taking care to leave enough water so that all the others may have at least a few drops. Thank the Elements, the Goddess and the God in the usual way and tidy up after yourself. Lastly, take your reserved water and give all your other plants a small amount.

Of course, gardening in pots and containers is not just for those with little or no outdoor space. Pots can also be utilized if you are not able to alter an existing garden. Perhaps you are living with others or are renting, or you feel that you will be likely to move in the not too distant future and would like to take your garden with you. Not only that, but elevating your plants in pots can enhance any garden, giving the illusion of more depth and space. Pots can also be used to confine rapid-growing or spreading plants.

TEN

PLANTS FOR MAGIC

In the Craft we call things that are linked one with another 'correspondences', that is, they correspond to one another. We also believe that everyone should work towards developing their own correspondences, as the links which are personally meaningful, rather than selected by someone else, will work better for each of us. For example, if you are working magic for Jill, her birth sign may indicate the plant lavender, but you know that she hates the smell and the colour. In these circumstances you may choose to give her a pink rose, which you know is her favourite. Alternatively, if you feel that her Goddess aspect is strongly linked to sunflowers, then you might plant them as a plant spell for her.

The following are by no means extensive lists of plant correspondences, but they do give a starting point and some ideas of ways you can link what you plant to reflect differing aspects of life and the Craft.

Please be aware that a good many of these plants are poisonous if eaten. Unless it says otherwise, their inclusion in these lists is intended to indicate that they can be grown to enhance the attributions mentioned, not consumed!

PLANTS ASSOCIATED WITH THE DEITIES

The Goddess as Maiden	Anemone, apple, artemesia, bay, crocus, daisy, hyacinth, marjoram, moonwort, myrtle, parsley, periwinkle, quince, rose, St John's wort, violet, willow.
The Goddess as Mother	Catnip, coltsfoot, crocus, heather, iris, myrtle, poppy, rose, sunflower, vervain. All night-flowering and evening scented flowers, such as night-scented stock, moon-daisies.
The Goddess as Crone	Belladonna, dandelion, fungi, garlic, hemlock, larkspur, lavender, lily, monkshood.
The God as Hunter	Artemesia, bay, cornflower, dogwood, evening primrose, garlic, hawthorn, mistletoe, rue, vervain, yarrow.
The Oak Lord	Apple, barley, corn, ivy, oak, wheat.
The Holly Lord	Evergreens, holly, mistletoe.
Sun Gods	Apple, bay, chrysanthemum, dogwood, goldenseal, heliotrope, hyacinth, sunflower.

GODDESSES LINKED TO PARTICULAR PLANTS

Ceres	Goddess of fertility in the fields.
Chloris	Goddess of all beautiful flowers, especially the rose.
Cybele	Goddess of nature and fertility, especially the pine.
Demeter	Goddess of grain.
Eostar	Saxon Goddess of fertility and spring, e.g. myrtle.
Flora	Goddess of flowers and fruit trees.
Iris	Goddess of the … iris!
Nyx	Goddess of all night-blooming flowers.
Pomona	Goddess of fruits and fertility.
Rhea	Goddess of the Earth, e.g. oak.

GODS LINKED TO PARTICULAR PLANTS

Attis	God of fertility and vegetation, e.g. almond.
Dionysus	God of apples, figs, grapes, and of course wine!
Faunus	God of nature, woodlands and fertility, e.g. bay.
Hyacinthus	God of Spring flowers, especially the hyacinth.
Lugh	God of corn and grain.
Min	Egyptian God of herbs of fertility.
Osiris	God of vegetation, e.g. ivy.
Pan	God of woodlands and fields.
Sylvanus	God of forests and fields.

THE ELEMENTS

Earth	Bulbs, honesty, honeysuckle, magnolia, pea, quince, roots, tubers, tulip.
Air	Borage, broom, caraway, clover, dandelion, eyebright, goldenrod, lavender, marjoram, mint, mistletoe, parsley, sage, summer savory.
Fire	Angelica, basil, bay, carrot, cat's-tail, coriander, dill, fennel, holly, lovage, marigold, rosemary, sunflower.
Water	Cabbage, chamomile, crocus, daisy, foxglove, groundsel, jasmine, lettuce, lily, poppy, sweet pea, tansy, watercress.
Spirit	Belladonna, cinquefoil, columbine, damiana, foxglove, hemlock, henbane, larkspur, lobelia, morning glory, passionflower, skullcap, thorn apple, valerian, wild lettuce, wormwood.

PLANTS ASSOCIATED WITH THE SABBATS

Samhain, 31 October	Apple, broom, ferns, heather, mint, nightshade, pumpkin, sage, wormwood.
Yule/Winter Solstice, 21 December	Ash, bay, chamomile, evergreens, holly, mistletoe, oak, rosemary, sage, thistle.
Imbolg, 2 February	Angelica, basil, bay, bramble, broom, celandine, heather, tansy, violet, wisteria.
Oestara/Spring Equinox, 21 March	Bluebell, celandine, cinquefoil, crocus, daffodil, dandelion, forsythia, gorse, honeysuckle, iris, jasmine, primrose, sage, tansy.
Beltane, 1 May	Angelica, bluebell, clover, cowslip, daisy, hawthorn, ivy, lilac, marigold, meadowsweet, primrose, rose, sorrel, woodruff.
Litha/Summer Solstice, 21 June	Chamomile, chicory, elder, fennel, larkspur, lavender, meadowsweet, St John's wort, thyme, wisteria, vervain.
Lughnasadh/Lammas, 1 August	Blackberry, corn, cyclamen, heather, hollyhock, poppy, sunflower.
Madron/Autumn Equinox, 21 September	Aster, chrysanthemum, fern, honeysuckle, marigold, passiflora, poppy, rose, sage, thistle.

PLANTS FOR THE SENSES

Our senses are linked to the Elements, and plants which appeal to our senses can also be used to develop our understanding of the Elements.

Hearing	Look for plants which move and rustle in the wind. Bamboo is an obvious, if somewhat exotic, choice, but as it is native in very few parts of the world why not also consider: Bulrushes (if you have a pond or very damp area), couch grass, fennel, goldenrod, honesty, hops, lavender (when the flowers have run to seed), witch grass.
Smell	Highly scented plants are always a boon in the garden. Some of my favourites are: Fennel, honeysuckle, jasmine, lavender, rosemary. It is worth noting that strong-smelling plants can also perform a different function: plants like chive, garlic, onion, rosemary, etc, help to deter pests.
Taste	There are many edible plants and herbs of which you will already be aware, but have you also thought of growing and eating: Marigold leaves, nasturtium flowers and leaves, rose petals, soapwort flowers, violet petals, wild strawberries. There are many other plants in this category, and *Herbs and Healing Plants* by Dieter Podlech, mentioned in the booklist (Appendix III), gives a lot of useful information on this, as do many other books of interest.
Touch	Seek out plants with an interesting texture, those with leaves covered with soft hairs, or non-stinging prickles: Asparagus, dandelion (when the heads have gone to seed), fennel, milk thistle, soapwort (another interesting and tactile plant as the leaves can be used in place of soap), teasels.
Sight	All plants are visual but some are more obvious than others, also it is good to have one or two which flower at night. Those with white or very pale blooms will seem to glow in moonlight, for example.

PLANTS ASSOCIATED WITH THE PLANETS

The planets have many correspondences of their own, including being associated with different kinds of magic.

The Sun	Magic related to power, success and the male principal. Bay, chamomile, eyebright, marigold, peony, rosemary, rue, St John's wort, sunflower.
The Moon	Divination, dreams, fertility, emotions, instinct, the female principal. Camellia, clary sage, dog rose, gardenia, honesty, jasmine, lily, lemon balm, mallow, moonwort, periwinkle, poppy, speedwell.
Mercury	Thought, communication, knowledge, speech, instruction. Beans, clover, dill, fennel, fern, lavender, lemongrass, lily of the valley, marjoram, mint, parsley, peppermint, savory.
Venus	Friendship, romance, love, beauty, self-respect, harmony, sympathy. Apple, blackberry, cat mint, catnip, coltsfoot, crocus, daffodil, daisy, damiana, feverfew, foxglove, heather, lilac, pea, primrose, rose, sweet pea, thyme, valerian.
Mars	Self-assertion, power, aggression, defence, discord, vitality. Anemone, basil, coriander, garlic, hawthorn, holly, hops, leek, onion, snapdragon, thistle.
Jupiter	Expansion, ambition, career, wealth, lust, law, justice, hope. Bay, borage, clove, comfrey, dandelion, honeysuckle, hyssop, lilac, sage, witch grass.
Saturn	Discipline, control, study, position. Belladonna, comfrey, henbane, horsetail, morning glory, pansy, quince, wolf's-bane.

Uranus	Independence, breaking free, changing habits. Acacia, ash, mimosa, pine.
Neptune	Refinement, sensitivity, uncertainty, illusion. All marsh and water plants.
Pluto	Transformation, rebirth, science, psychic powers. Dog rose, mint, peppermint.

PLANTS ASSOCIATED WITH THE ZODIAC
(SUN SIGNS)

Aries	Carnation, deer's tongue, fennel, peppermint.
Taurus	Daisy, honeysuckle, lilac, orchid, thyme, violet.
Gemini	Bergamot, clover, dill, horehound, lavender, mint.
Cancer	Gardenia, jasmine, lemon balm, rose, violet.
Leo	Heliotrope, juniper, nutmeg, rosemary, sunflower.
Virgo	Bergamot, fennel, honeysuckle, lily, mint, moss.
Libra	Apple blossom, catnip, mugwort, sweet pea, vanilla.
Scorpio	Basil, deer's tongue, gardenia, ginger, violet.
Sagittarius	Carnation, honeysuckle, orange, sage.
Capricorn	Magnolia, mimosa, oak moss, vervain.
Aquarius	Acacia, lavender, mimosa, peppermint.
Pisces	Cat mint, gardenia, jasmine, sage, sweet pea.

MAGICAL PURPOSES

Beauty	Catnip, maidenhair, rose.
Courage	Borage, sweet pea, thyme.
Divination	Broom, dandelion, goldenrod.

Fertility	Carrot, cyclamen, daffodil, poppy.
Friendship	Passionflower, sweet pea.
Happiness	Catnip, hawthorn, lily of the valley, witch grass.
Healing	Angelica, bay, cowslip, fennel, hops, mint, rosemary, violet.
Health	Fern, geranium, marjoram, St John's wort, tansy, thyme.
Love	Basil, chamomile, columbine, lavender, lemon balm, periwinkle, rose, wormwood.
Luck	Bluebell, daffodil, heather, poppy, strawberry.
Mental powers	Caraway, lily of the valley, rosemary, summer savory.
Money	Basil, blackberry, honesty, moss, poppy, snapdragon, violet.
Peace and harmony	Lavender, morning glory, passionflower, vervain.
Protection of the home	Garlic, hydrangea, primrose, rowan, thistle, vetivert, witch grass.
Protection of people	Comfrey, hyacinth, lavender, lemongrass, snapdragon, witch hazel, wolf's-bane.
Psychic powers	Bay, honeysuckle, lemongrass, marigold, thyme, wormwood.
Purification	Broom, chamomile, fennel, lavender, parsley, valerian.
Relaxation and sleep	Chamomile, hops, lavender, lettuce, valerian, vervain.
Strength	Bay, St John's wort, thistle.
Success	Lemon balm, clover, rowan.

ELEVEN

LUNAR GARDENING AND PLANT CARE

It has long been known that the Moon has influence over the growth of plants. Planting and tending according to the lunar phases and its position in the heavens are among the oldest of gardening techniques. To make the most of this information you will need to acquire an ephemeris or a diary giving detailed information on the position of the Moon within the Zodiac. Of course, you will also have to take into account the seasons and the weather: no matter how propitious the Moon, putting seedlings into frozen ground is almost certain to fail!

THE PHASES OF THE MOON

The phases of the Moon are one of the key cycles of the Craft. The Moon is seen as reflecting the Aspects of the Triple Goddess: the Maiden at the New Moon, the Mother at the Full, and the Crone at the Waning Moon. These Aspects relate directly to everything in our lives and to the magics we work: the New Moon for beginnings, the Full Moon for fruitfulness and growth, the Waning Moon for wisdom, rest and ridding ourselves of the unwanted.

Not only that, but we utilize the tides of the Moon: the Waxing for increase and growth and the Waning for decrease and banishing. It is traditional to use these tides for planting, with those things which grow above the ground being planted during the Waxing Moon, and those which grow below being planted at the Waning.

The Moon's phases are often referred to in terms of Quarters and each of these has its beneficial attributes for different gardening activities:

First Quarter

Increasing from the New Moon to the half. A time to plant annuals which produce above the ground such as leafy plants, herbs, grains, and those which produce their seed outside the plant. Cucumber is an exception to this and should be planted during the first quarter. Sow seeds. Plant spells for new starts and beginnings.

Second Quarter

Increasing from the Half Moon to the Full. Plant annuals that produce their seed inside the fruit and climbing plants. Collect herbs for use in recipes or spells for increase. Plant spells for healing, increase, fertility and to bring balance.

Third Quarter

Decreasing from the Full Moon to the half. Plant biennials, perennials, bulbs, root plants, trees and shrubs. If, however, you have little space and are trying to limit the growth of trees and shrubs then plant them in the fourth quarter. Pick herbs intended for spells and remedies which drive things out or away. Plant spells for reducing things or driving them away.

Fourth Quarter

Decreasing from the half to just before the New. A time for destroying weeds, dealing with pests, trimming or mowing to slow growth. Dig over the soil, make repairs to structures such as fences, etc. Cut herbs for divination and meditation spells. Plant spells for stopping bad habits, etc.

Many people find that following these phases, when growing fruit and vegetables, results in not only a bigger crop but also better tasting foods. Herbs, too, will have a greater potency if planted and picked at the appropriate times. Of course, there will be times when you cannot follow these guidelines – this does not mean your plants will not grow, but that they may not grow so well.

USING THE GARDEN IN TUNE WITH THE MOON'S PHASES

Your garden should not just be a place of work, either physical or magical. Following the phases of the Moon it can be a place where you can recharge your batteries and enhance your life. Each of the following short meditations is intended to let you do just that. In each of them you will need to spend just a few minutes outside at a time when the Moon is visible in the sky, to take advantage of the energy of the Moon and the land.

NEW MOON

Make a point of going out into your garden when the first sliver of the Moon appears in the sky. Remind yourself that this is a time of new starts and fresh beginnings, a time to be optimistic about what is to come. If possible, take off your shoes and let your bare feet come into contact with the Earth. Close your eyes and visualize the Maiden, full of youthful energy. Visualize also the growth in the land, feel this energy rising up through your feet and filling you with new life and hope.

FIRST QUARTER, THE WAXING MOON

At the growing half Moon the tidal increase in the Moon's energy is at its swiftest. Sit and place your hands and bare feet on the earth, look up to the Moon and let your mind feel the pulse of the land and the energy all around. Visualize becoming a part of the land and letting the energies of the elements and the Moon flow through you, to cleanse and empower you.

FULL MOON

Many Witches like to 'Moon bathe', that is, lie naked in the Moonlight, at this time. This may be possible outdoors if your garden is very secluded, and the weather warm, but most of us make do with lying on our own bed with the window open! Alternatively, dress in something loose and unrestricting and with naked feet go out into your garden. Take a few minutes to gaze up at the Moon – if you direct your gaze just above it you will avoid compromising your night-sight. Visualize the Goddess as Mother, dressed in flowing robes and sweeping across the night sky. Feel her energy in the Moonlight pouring down on you. Breathe deeply to absorb as much as you need.

THIRD QUARTER, THE WANING MOON

At the decreasing half Moon remember that all things must be allowed to pass. This is a time to let go of outworn thoughts and feelings, resentments, quarrels and spent emotions.

DARK OF MOON

During the three days just before the New Moon, there is no Moon visible in the sky. Remind yourself that, like the Moon, we all need times of rest in order to be whole and give of our best in everyday life. When you go indoors again, make a point of doing something relaxing which you enjoy, something purely for yourself.

THE MOON'S ZODIACAL POSITION

The Moon passes through all of the twelve Zodiacal signs every 28 or so days, spending around two days in each, in the same way as the Sun does throughout the year. Each of the signs has attributes which you can use to enhance your spells and remedies. If, however, the need is urgent, do not wait until the Moon is in the 'right' place, but give some thought as to whether you need to repeat the action at the next appropriate time.

Aries   Destroy pests and weeds. Turn over the soil. Plant spells for defence or to settle quarrels. Harvest herbs and create remedies for the mind and thought processes.

Taurus   Plant root crops, lettuce, cabbage and leafy vegetables. Plant spells for protection of the home and family. Harvest herbs and create remedies for insect repellent sachets and other protective purposes.

Gemini   Destroy pests and weeds. Turn over the soil. Plant spells for communication and mental powers. Harvest herbs and create remedies for the respiratory and nervous system.

Cancer   Plant crops, herbs and anything you intend to harvest, especially if the seeds are your target. Plant spells for home, family and relationships. Harvest herbs and create remedies for digestive troubles.

Leo   Destroy pests and weeds. Turn over the soil. Plant spells for self-expression, assertiveness, increased energy and employment-related difficulties. Harvest herbs and create remedies for the heart and circulation.

Virgo   Destroy pests and weeds. Turn over the soil. Plant spells for fertility, study and anything requiring attention to detail. Harvest herbs and create remedies for the alimentary tract.

Libra	Plant root crops and anything with fleshy leaves or stems. Also those plants whose flowers and fruits you wish to promote. Plant spells for balance and justice. Harvest herbs and create remedies for the kidneys and bladder.
Scorpio	Plant anything you wish to harvest, especially vines. Also any plants you wish to encourage to a sturdy or stocky growth. Plant spells for psychic energies, transformation and those related to enhancing your Craft. Harvest herbs and create remedies for the reproductive system.
Sagittarius	Plant onions, garlic, grass and hay. Plant spells for understanding and for healing animals. Harvest herbs and create remedies for the liver and general sluggish or lethargic feelings.
Capricorn	Plant root crops and potatoes. Plant spells for restraint and discipline and to prevent friends, partners or pets from straying. Harvest herbs and create remedies for the bones and joints.
Aquarius	Destroy pests and weeds. Turn over the soil. Plant spells to increase intuition, understanding and divination. Harvest herbs and create remedies for the circulatory system and problems of the blood.
Pisces	Plant moisture-loving and pond plants. Plant spells for artistic inspiration and healing. Harvest herbs and create remedies for emotional problems.

If you have had an Astrological Birth Chart done, then have a look at the sign the Moon was in at your birth. This is the best time to plant spells for personal growth and development, regardless of the above.

GENERAL GUIDELINES FOR PLANT CARE

Although this is not a standard book on gardening, I have included here a few tips and hints for plant care. Plants have their preferred living conditions: different soil types, amounts of sunlight or shade, different amounts of water and so on. If your plant, seeds or whatever come with instructions, read them! Not every plant is the same, and these days even one cultivar may vary considerably from its cousins.

HOUSING

✦ Turn over or loosen soil at least once a year. This allows air and water to penetrate and garden friends like worms to do their work for you.

✦ Pot plants do better in a pot which is not too small or too big. Too small and there's no room for the roots. Too large and the plant will put its energy into growing root and stem, not flowers and foliage.

✦ Use potting compost for pot plants, as garden soil often contains weeds and pests, and may not be nutritious enough.

WATERING

✦ Plants, including houseplants, prefer rainwater, unless highly polluted. Keep a vessel outside which will collect rainwater.

✦ Water from the base, rather than the top, whenever you can.

★ Houseplants benefit from being given a deep bath once a year. Place them in water deep enough to come two-thirds of the way up the pot and leave for an hour. Do not plunge them into an icy bath if it is a hot day, let the water stand before adding the plants. Drain well before moving, or there'll be muddy drips all over the floor!

★ All but the most sensitive houseplants will benefit from standing out in a mild Spring shower or two.

★ Try not to get drops of water on flowers and foliage if it is in bright sunlight, as water droplets act like little magnifiers and will cause burnt patches. It is better to water in the morning before the Sun gets too hot, or at sundown.

★ Over-watering is as bad as under-watering. Even in the same room some plants will need more water than others. Always test a pot plant's soil by placing your finger on it to see if it is damp.

FEEDING

★ Plants like to be fed just before and during the growing season, but rarely all year round.

★ Always follow the instructions on plant food and remember, more is not better.

PROBLEMS

Slugs and Snails

★ Throwing slugs and snails over the fence is pointless, not only will it upset your neighbours, but they actually return home!

★ A border of sand around the edge of your property will discourage slugs and snails from entering, but will also prevent those inside from leaving so you might want to relocate them to some wasteland. Pots can be protected by gluing a band of sandpaper around them.

✫ Alternatively, place petroleum jelly onto strips of paper; neither slugs nor snails like to cross this barrier.

Bugs and Pests

✫ A good many pests can be removed by spraying with soapy water: use a little washing-up liquid in the water.

✫ Natural enemies are the best way of keeping pests under control and a small woodpile is a good way of attracting the kinds of beetles, etc, which feed on pests.

✫ Strong-smelling plants like garlic, chives and onions deter many pests, so grow them in amongst your other plants. Summer savory is particularly good at deterring aphids.

✫ Keep an old toothbrush for removing the more persistent bugs.

✫ There are now several companies which sell ecological and even live pest controls. Most garden centres can advise you on the best for your problem.

✫ Indoor plants can often be 'treated' by placing them in the bath and giving them a fairly strong shower, with cold water.

Cats and Dogs

✫ Both cats and dogs like to mark the boundaries of their property. If you can, see where the marking places are and plant delicate things elsewhere.

✫ If the pets in question are yours do try to ensure that there is an acceptable area for them. Dogs can be trained to use such a space by the reward system. As cats will often return to use the same spot, you can encourage them by moving some of the soil and faeces (wear gloves and use an old shovel) and placing it in your preferred location.

✫ Fresh orange, lemon and grapefruit peel can work as a deterrent to some cats and dogs, and as a last resort a long-range water pistol can be very effective!

Children

★ Children can be encouraged to respect your plants if they have some of their own to grow. Chapter 12 talks about children's gardening.

TWELVE

THE MAGIC PRIMER

If we want our children to grow up to understand the cycles of the seasons, to love nature and respect the land, we need to start them early. If we want them to respect our plants we need to give them an understanding of why these things are important to us. Many parents come to me and ask how they can include their young in elements of the Craft, and nowhere is it easier than when working in the garden. Even very tiny children enjoy the magic of a germinating seed, or seeing whose sunflower will grow tallest.

Growing vegetables is even more fun, as they get to eat the results! From the perspective of a parent, enlisting the help of youngsters not only gets the garden chores done more rapidly, but it is an opportunity to share time doing 'grown up' things. As a bonus, it also gets them off the computer, away from the TV and gives them some fresh air which may, if you are lucky, result in a child who is prepared to go to sleep at bedtime!

If you can, give over a portion of your garden to your child, so that they have their own patch to tend. Don't expect this to be an area you do not have to look after, as even the best junior gardener will need help from time to time. To encourage regular watering of plants, buy a separate, cheap watering can and allow them to decorate it with paint, glue, shells, feathers or whatever takes their imagination. Resist the temptation to give them an inconspicuous corner, as if it's out of the way it will just be easier for them to forget! Also, be fair, don't hand over that nasty patch where you can't get anything to grow. My first garden was a really grotty place under a rhododendron bush and nearly put me off for life.

Find a reasonable place and, before handing it over, prepare it well. Dig it over and remove weeds, large rocks and stones, and give the soil a boost by digging in some compost, too. Encourage them to mark the border of their patch with stones, shells or something similar, anything to encourage a sense of ownership and involvement. One useful idea is to give them the 'leading edge' of a flowerbed. Not only does this mean that their patch will be well within their reach but, carefully selected, you might find that footballs, etc, are not kicked onto your plants, if they have to pass through theirs first.

PLANTS FOR CHILDREN

Plants which are good for children have two main identifying criteria: they should be non-toxic, as even the most cautious children may put their fingers in their mouth during or after gardening, and they should preferably grow relatively fast or develop rapidly; as children are generally less patient than adults. So choose fast-sprouting seeds or purchase plants which are just about to bloom. The following is a selection of some children's favourites.

Runner beans	These grow fairly fast and should be trained upwards. They have beautiful red flowers and children love hunting amongst the leaves for the beans.
Carrots	These grow rapidly from seed and will produce tiny carrots which are very sweet. When you use carrots in the kitchen you can also place the top in a saucer of water and a bushy green plant will soon emerge.

Cornflowers	These will grow rapidly from seed and are a beautiful blue. Do be aware that they are self-seeding and if not managed will pop up all over the garden!
Evening primrose	Easy to grow and has masses of yellow flowers that last for ages. It can become quite large, so give it space, or keep it trimmed.
Heartsease or wild pansy	Used to be called 'three faces under a hood'. It grows fairly fast and will produce a stunning display of flowers. Children love the way the heads face down in rain and at night, making it look as though it is shy.
Heather	A friend recommended this to me as being easy to grow, although, it's one of those plants that I never seem to have any luck with! If you do get it to do well, it has many uses and can provide hours of fun. Dry it and put it into little pillow bags with lavender, or sometimes with rose petals. It can be used as an antiseptic and its scent has a calming effect. The dried flowers have been used to make tea and the roots to flavour beers.
Lavender	If you buy a small plant early in the year, it will flower the same summer.
Marigolds	Rapid growers with bright flowers, you need to keep them in check as they can take over. The flowers and leaves can be eaten in salad or added to fish dishes. There's more on marigolds in Chapter 7.
Nasturtiums	Another rapid grower with brilliant flowers, and also mentioned in Chapter 7. Likes plenty of water and will flower all year if the conditions are right. Deters slugs and snails on neighbouring plants. Again the flowers and leaves can be eaten.
Poppies	They grow quickly and if you dead-head them they will continue to flower through the summer. They're very hardy and will readily forgive if not watered!
Radishes	They grow fast and can be used to make 'radish flowers' as a garnish or table decoration. Cut slits into a radish, submerge it in cold water and it will open out.

Snapdragons	Not the fastest of growers but the flowers make instant 'finger puppets' and when I was young we called them 'bunny rabbits'!
Sunflowers	The all-time children's favourite. They shoot up fast, and grow really tall. They have huge flowers and the seeds can be collected, cooked and eaten, or used to feed the birds. Sunflowers will turn their heads to follow the Sun's path across the sky.
Sweet peas	They grow rapidly from seed and can be trained upwards.

Of course, not every plant in a child's patch needs to be a rapid grower. It's a good idea to also have one or two scented plants and an evergreen or two so that it doesn't look barren in winter. Rosemary combines both these qualities in one plant.

SEASONAL FUN

One of the ways of interesting children in the Wheel of the Year is to introduce activities which reflect the seasons, and the growth in the garden.

SAMHAIN

It wouldn't be Halloween without making a pumpkin lantern. Let your child draw the face on, but you wield the knife! Make the most of the plentiful supply of apples by apple bobbing, either in a bowl of water outside or by suspending apples from strings indoors. Make home-made toffee apples. Thread unshelled peanuts onto a string and hang it up for the birds. Fill empty yoghurt pots with a blend of birdseed, fat and bread-crumbs and hang upside down for tits and other agile birds to eat.

YULE

Collect fir cones and decorate them with paint, glue and glitter, and use them as a part of the Yule and Christmas decorations.

Make a 'Christmas Tree' for the birds, either use an existing tree or by pushing a long branch into the soil and hanging peanut strings, fat balls and other bird feeders from it.

IMBOLG

Try to visit a children's farm to see the new lambs – it may be safest to phone ahead and check there are some! Look along verges and in churchyards for the first snowdrops. Be sure to point out the first buds and shoots of Spring. Young children can be encouraged to make 'candles' from the centres of loo rolls and some red paper 'flames'.

OESTARA

Organize an egg hunt in the garden. It's probably best to use mini eggs for this, to prevent an excess of chocolate being eaten. Decorate hard-boiled eggs with food colouring and safe felt-tip pens. Make daisy chains and remember to do the 'buttercup test'! Look out for hares in the fields.

BELTANE

Keep an eye out for the first may or hawthorn blossom. Look for bluebells and primroses in the woods, but remember not to tread on the leaves as it harms the plants. Look for the catkins of hazel too. Make a maypole as described in Chapter 8 or weave garlands of flowers to hang in the house.

LITHA

Collect some oak leaves and make a Green Man mask using a paper plate. Cut eye and mouth holes and put ties on both sides.

Go to a 'Pick Your Own' farm to gather fruit. If you can manage it, go at the beginning, height and end of the season to see the different stages of the crop.

Create a human sundial. Place a flat stone at the 'centre' for standing on, then use the passage of the Sun to mark out the hours with numbered rocks or pebbles.

LUGHNASADH

Use corn stalks to make corn 'dolls' of all shapes and sizes. Make gingerbread men which children can decorate with edible bits and pieces. Or bake bread in harvest shapes. Gather lavender tops, heather flowers, rose petals and sprigs of rosemary, dry them thoroughly and make into little 'cushions' which can be placed under the pillow, in the drawers or simply hung around the house. Seek out a Maize Maze to walk through.

MADRON

Go brambling to pick blackberries. Look for a sweet chestnut tree and collect the nuts. These can be pealed and eaten – they taste sweeter if cooked but are still quite edible raw. Horse chestnuts can also be collected and used for conker battles, but mind your knuckles! Find a magnifying glass and go on a bug hunt. You may find it helpful to borrow a field guide from the local library to help in identification. Grow mustard and cress on saucers in the kitchen.

At each of the festivals make a point of showing your children the changes in the garden since the previous one. Create a seasonal scrapbook with pressed flowers and herbs, and possibly a photograph from each Sabbat. Try also to take a walk through your nearest green space, or along a country lane, at each Sabbat, where you can see wild flowers and plants and get new ideas for your own garden.

Of course, if you really want to engender a love of nature in your young, make time to have fun together in outdoor spaces. Not only will it benefit them, but it's also a great way of relieving stress and getting away from that nagging feeling that you should be doing the housework!

WHAT WITCHCRAFT REALLY IS!

itchcraft may be one of the faster growing spiritual belief systems in the world today, but there are still a lot of misconceptions and prejudices surrounding it. Some have been generated by modern films, books and TV programmes; these portray the Craft as anything from glamorous and fun, to a satanic devil worship of the worst kind. Other prejudices, and even fears, have a deeper origin in the propaganda of the Church of Rome which sought to superimpose its faith, along with taxation and political control, on the beliefs of rest of the world. As a result the perception of many people is confused, to say the least.

The following is a brief introduction to Witchcraft, as it really is, and as it is practised by millions of people in the world today.

Witchcraft is one of a number of belief systems whose roots pre-date Christianity and which come under the 'umbrella' heading of Pagan. Indeed, Witchcraft has roots which go back to Palaeolithic times, as illustrated by the cave paintings of our ancient ancestors. Having said that, the Craft is a living religion and has as much relevance to us today as it had to its practitioners in the past. We still seek healing of our bodies and minds, strength to deal with our daily lives, understanding and compassion to help us relate to those around us, and to develop ourselves.

So what do Witches believe and how do they express their beliefs? First, you have to understand that, unlike the more 'orthodox' religions, the Craft has no paid or formal

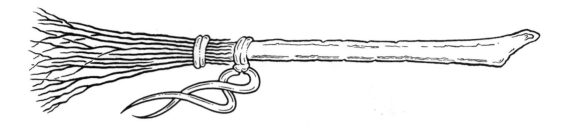

priesthood; in the Craft we are each our own Priest or Priestess and therefore make our own decisions as to the expression of our beliefs. As a result there is no 'one true way' to being a Witch. This gives rise to a great diversity in our daily practices, and indeed enables the Craft to grow and adapt to the real world in a way that other paths find difficult because of their interpreted doctrine. Having said that, there are many beliefs and practices that most Witches hold in common.

WE BELIEVE THAT THE DIVINE IS BOTH MALE AND FEMALE

We believe that the Divine is male and female in perfect balance, and that we should seek that balance in ourselves and in our lives. Put simply, this means that we believe in the Goddess and the God, and they may be referred to by many names, according to the needs of the individual or indeed their personal preference. It helps to think of the Divine as being like a mirror ball, with each facet having a different identity, although all being part of the Divine. As a result you may find that the Goddess is referred to as, for example, Isis, Astarte or Hecate, and the God referred to as, perhaps, Osiris, Herne or Pan. Some Witches will simply refer to the Lord and Lady or the Goddess and the God, others will call them the Old Ones or the Old Gods, or even just the Gods.

The Goddess is seen as having three aspects: Maiden, Mother and Crone (or Wise One). These aspects are reflected in the cycle of the Moon, and in our daily lives, for everything has its beginning, middle and closing phases. The God also has different aspects, but these are more clearly defined through the festivals of the seasons and the Wheel of the Year.

WE ARE EACH OUR OWN PRIEST OR PRIESTESS

As mentioned above we have no formal Priesthood in the Craft, although those Witches working in a group or Coven setting will have a High Priestess and High Priest who are the leaders of that group. This does not make them better Witches; it simply denotes their standing and authority within that group. Having no formal priesthood means we do not rely on others to interpret or intercede with our Gods for us, we are each entitled to make our own connection with the Divine, in our own way. This might be through ritual, meditation and/or magic, and most Witches will use a combination of different techniques at different times.

WE HAVE NO 'BOOK OF INSTRUCTION'

There is nothing written in Witchcraft in the way that Christians have the Bible or Muslims the Koran. There are a great number of books on the Craft and it is up to those who wish to read some of these and make personal decisions as to their relevance. Each individual can choose the complexity of their Rituals, and the form that their path will take. For some this may mean working in a group or Coven, while others may prefer a solitary path. Some will seek to work formalized magic whilst others prefer the Hedgewitch approach, working closely with nature and using herbs to achieve their magics.

EVERYONE IS ENTITLED TO THEIR OWN, INFORMED CHOICE OF SPIRITUAL PATH, SO LONG AS THEY HARM NO ONE ELSE

Witchcraft is a non-proselytizing belief system; we do not feel the need for everyone to believe as we do in order to feel secure in our faith. There is plenty of room in this world for everyone to find their own way of relating to the Divine. In fact, all religions have as much, if not more, in common than in difference. Hence there is no reason why we should not encourage and celebrate a diversity of beliefs. As Witches we encourage our young to examine many paths and to make their own decisions, based on their own needs. We do not seek to convert others to our beliefs, but neither do we wish to be indoctrinated in turn.

WE BELIEVE THAT WE SHOULD RESPECT NATURE

This means not taking more than we need and indeed trying to recompense for that which we have taken. This involves trying to live, not only in the modern world, but also in balance with the planet. Witches tend to shop second hand, make at least some of the things they use and to recycle where they can. This does not mean that we are all 'green warriors' campaigning against the building of roads or houses. It does mean that we try to tread lightly on the world.

WITCHES UTILIZE THE ELEMENTS IN THEIR WORKINGS

It is not just that we respect nature, we also see ourselves reflected by the elements of Air, Fire, Water, Earth and Spirit. Whilst these elements are all around us in nature they are also within us; Air is our thoughts, Fire is our passions and enthusiasm, Water is our emotions, Earth is our bodies, and Spirit is our inner selves. These are the energies we harness in working magic and in order for this to work effectively we must be able to achieve balance between them. These elements also have reflections in daily life. For every project to work it must have its phases of thought, enthusiasm, emotional involvement and formation, and must also be imbued with its own spirit. These elements are represented by the five-pointed star, or Pentagram, which when placed in a circle becomes the Pentacle worn by many Witches as a symbol of their beliefs.

WE BELIEVE IN AND PRACTISE MAGIC

Magic has been defined as the ability to create change by force of will and in some respects is not dissimilar to a belief in the power of prayer. However, in magic it is our personal intervention which creates the change around us. Magic is not like cookery, just a matter of following a recipe and getting a result. True magic requires a deep understanding of ourselves and the energies that are around us, and the ability to control and focus our own energies. One of the greatest keys to this is the ability to visualize. It also requires a study and understanding of the elements of Earth, Air, Fire and Water, not just in the world, but also within us. The magic we practise is not that of stage conjuring or of the special effects that you see so often in modern films. It is practised to heal, protect and enhance our lives. It is worked for ourselves, our near and dear, and for those who come to us with requests for help. Magic should always be practised with the Wiccan Rede in mind and also with regard to the law of threefold return which states that whatever you do, good or ill, will be returned to you three times over. This latter is not confined to magical working, but should be borne in mind at all times. There are other concerns which should be taken into account before starting any magical working and these are detailed in *The Real Witches' Handbook*. However, if you are careful to harm no one and not to interfere with anyone's freedom of will, then you have the basic guidelines for good magical practice.

WITCHES CELEBRATE THE WHEEL OF THE YEAR

The Witches' calendar contains eight key festivals, called Sabbats. At these we mark the changes of the seasons and the stories of the Goddess and the God. Whenever possible Witches will gather together to celebrate these festivals. We dance, sing and honour the Goddess and the God by re-enactment of their stories. Solitary Witches also mark the Sabbats, and ways of doing this can also be found in *The Real Witches' Handbook*. At the end of these rituals we celebrate by feasting with food and wines. Many of the Sabbats are familiar to non-Witches as they have been taken over by newer belief systems and incorporated into their calendars.

The Sabbats are:

Samhain	31 October. The most important festival of the year. The beginning and end of the year, the beginning of the resting season of the land and a time of remembrance of those who have gone before. A feast of the Goddess as Crone and Wise One.
Yule	21 December. The Winter Solstice, when the decreasing length of daylight gives way to increasing light, and we celebrate the rebirth of the Sun.
Imbolg	2 February. When the first signs of life are seen returning to the land. When the Goddess changes her robes of Crone for those of Maiden.
Oestara	21 March. The Spring Equinox, when day and night are equal. The festival of the Goddess Eostar, who is derived from the Goddess Astarte, and whose symbols are the egg and the hare.
Beltane	1 May. The second most important festival of the year. The Goddess changes her robes of Maiden for those of Mother and we celebrate the marriage of the Goddess and the God.
Litha	21 June. The Summer Solstice. Here the Sun is at the peak of its power, and the lengthening days are replaced by those growing shorter again.
Lughnasadh or Lammas	1 August. The festival of the first of the harvest. The feast of Lugh and of the Sacrificial King, who is these days most often represented by the gingerbread man.
Madron	21 September. The Autumn Equinox, once more a time of balance, when day and night are equal, and the feast of the height of the harvest.

On the return to Samhain the year has turned full circle, hence the term Wheel of the Year.

WE TAKE PERSONAL RESPONSIBILITY FOR OUR LIVES

The main 'rule' in the Craft is called the Wiccan Rede; 'An it harm none, do what thou will.' This in itself includes not only our respect for others and the world around us, but also respect for ourselves. We do not believe that we can blame external forces or other people for our thoughts, words and deeds, and that if we do wrong it is up to us to do our best to rectify it.

WE SEEK PERSONAL DEVELOPMENT

There is much to learn in the world and in the Craft, but we do not expect others to feed us this information. We actively seek to expand our knowledge and extend our skills by personal effort. All Witches are aware that they will never know enough, let alone all. This personal development also includes expanding our personal skills and attributes, 'ironing out' our personal misconceptions and problems, and each working to become the best self we possibly can. Witchcraft has been called, and rightly so in my opinion, 'a thinking person's belief system', as it involves a course of personal exploration and general study which never ceases.

THE SUMMERLANDS AND REINCARNATION

Witches believe that we live many lives and between them we return to the Summerlands, a resting place where we review the lessons we have learned in the life we have just completed, and select the lessons to be learned in the life to come. When we speak of reincarnation we do not mean that we come back as the same person but rather that our spirit is born again. Whilst it can be interesting to research previous incarnations, and the information we acquire may illuminate aspects of our current lives, it is necessary to remember that the personal responsibility we also believe in means that we cannot blame our past(s) for our current problems. We must live in the present and work towards achievement in this life.

WITCHES PRACTISE HERBLORE

We utilize the properties of plants and nature for healing and self-improvement, and in the course of our magic. Herbs, plants and spices can be used in food and drink, lotions and ointments, sachets and talismans, incenses and candles. They can be used in their natural state (as I write this I have rosemary on my desk to aid my thoughts and concentration), dried or in oil form, as in aromatherapy which has become so popular in recent years.

WITCHES CREATE OUR OWN SACRED SPACE

Witches do not have special buildings in which they worship, in fact most Witches do not have a room or even a space set aside for working. The Witch creates his or her own working space wherever and whenever it is needed, and this can be inside or out. This space is called the Circle, and it is created in several steps. Briefly speaking they are:

★ The invocation of the Elements of Air, Fire, Water and Earth, which are the energies on which we draw. They are always called in this order as Air represents thought, which should precede all our actions. We bring the Element of Spirit to the Circle through ourselves and through the Divine.

★ The invitation of the Goddess and the God: the Divine, whose assistance we need to perform our working, and in whose honour we gather.

★ The drawing of a Circle large enough to contain those taking part and the actions they are there to perform. This is usually done on the psychic level rather than on the physical, although some will place markers to visibly show the boundary. The Circle is drawn clockwise (or deosil) from the north-east point of the area, between Earth and Air, and overlaps at that point in order to ensure that it is complete. The Circle is there to contain the energy raised, until it is ready to be released, and to protect those within its boundaries from outside energies and distractions.

These steps can be formal and relatively elaborate in group working, or very simple and performed using visualization when created by a Solitary Witch. Any action which takes place within the Sacred Space will have more effect and potency than the same action performed outside of the Sacred Space. In addition, things can be made outside of the Circle and then taken into it to be magically enhanced or empowered, and then blessed and consecrated for use.

WITCHES AND WITCHCRAFT

There are many different branches of today's Craft:

* *Gardnerian* This tradition was founded by Gerald Gardner, who is sometimes known as the Father of Modern Witchcraft. Gardnerian Witchcraft is strongly based around Gerald Gardner's own *Book of Shadows* and his Rituals are closely adhered to.

* *Alexandrian* This branch of the Craft was founded by Alex and Maxine Sanders. It is less rigid and more flexible than Gardnerian Craft.

* *Hereditary* This, as the name indicates, is Witchcraft which is passed down from one generation to the next through the family line.

* *Traditional* This term relates to Witchcraft which is not so much learned as remembered. Traditional Witches are those for whom the Craft comes instinctively. They often work magic and understand the precepts before discovering Witchcraft.

* *Hedgewitch* These are Witches whose Craft is almost entirely based around the land and nature. They work almost exclusively through herbs and plants.

Witches may work within these traditions on their own as Solitaries, or in groups which are often called Covens.

The term Coven is used to describe a group of Witches who meet and work together on a regular basis. Despite the common misconception, a Coven does not have to be 13 people, but is essentially any number from three upwards. A Witch on his or her own is termed a Solitary Witch. Witches may be Solitary through choice – it can be easier to get things done if you don't have to take account of others – or because they are unable to locate a suitable Coven. Two Witches working together are usually termed a Partnership, even when of the same gender. More than two and it is termed a group or Coven. As with any group, the Coven has to have a leader and this is usually the High Priestess, either supported by the High Priest or on her own. In some cases a Coven will be run by the High Priest, but this is usually because there is no Priestess of sufficient rank and experience to take the role of High Priestess.

Just as there are many different kinds of Witch there are different kinds of Coven. There are Gardnerian, Alexandrian, Hereditary and Traditional Covens, and even some which combine these and other aspects of the Craft. There are even cyber-Covens, although unless very well directed, these tend to be more of a forum where Solitaries can share ideas, seek magical assistance and generally discuss the Craft. There are some Covens which are single sex, although the majority are mixed. Some are dedicated to specific pantheons of Gods; others are more eclectic. Some will take newcomers (often called Aspirants or Neophytes); some won't. Generally speaking, most Covens will initially follow the path that was learned by their High Priestess, although their practice will almost always evolve and differ from this in time. This is one of the reasons for the diversity of practice which can be found in the Craft. There is no 'right' type of Coven, but it is important to find, or create, the kind that is right for you.

Witches who have joined a Coven hold the same beliefs, celebrate the same festivals and work magic together. This is not to say that those in a Coven don't work on their own, but solitary work by Coven members is supported by the High Priestess and the rest of the Coven.

SEEK TO KNOW MORE?

If you would like to know more about today's Witchcraft I would recommend reading *The Real Witches' Handbook* and some of the other books mentioned in the Recommended Reading at the end of this book.

TERMS AND DEFINITIONS

Some of the words in here may have only been touched upon briefly in the text. However, they are words which are in common use in the Craft and may well crop up in other books you have read or will read. Other words are also in common usage but have a particular meaning within the Craft, and that is the meaning I have given here.

Annuals	Plants which complete their life cycle in one season and have to be grown again from seed each year. This is not as bad as it sounds as many annuals are self-seeding.
Asperger	A small bundle of twigs tied together to form a mini-brush. An asperger is used to sprinkle water, and sometimes oil, around an area.
Aspirant	A person who has joined the Coven and has taken their Coven Oath, but has yet to take their First Degree Initiation. These are sometimes referred to as Neophytes.
Athame	The Witches' knife or blade. Traditionally, a black-handled knife with a double-edged blade 9 inches (23 cm) long, the Athame is used when invoking and banishing the elements and other energies. The only thing an Athame should cut is air, or the wedding cake at a Handfasting. Some traditions hold that iron should not be taken into the Circle and hence, if they have an Athame it will not be made with that metal.
Besom	The traditional Witches' broomstick. This symbol of fertility is literally jumped during a Handfasting to signify the leap from one 'life' to the next. The besom is also used to symbolically sweep the circle.
Biennials	Plants which flower and fruit only in their second year, and which then die.
Boline	The white-handled knife. This is the working knife of the Witch and is used whenever any cutting, say of herbs, or carving of symbols is required.
Book of Shadows	A personal record or journal of all your magical workings, and the thoughts, feelings and results that come from them. Gardnerian Witches refer to *The Book of Shadows* which was written by Gerald Gardner together with some of his senior Coven members.

Candidate	A person who wishes to join the Coven, about whom the High Priestess has yet to make a decision. Some Candidates may be Initiates, where they have self-initiated, or in some cases the Initiates of other Covens.
Censer	A heatproof container for burning incense. A censer usually has a perforated lid, to let the heat and vapours out, and chains so that it can be hung from a convenient hook, or even swung so that you can circulate the perfume.
Chalice	The Chalice is a symbol of the Goddess and can be made from wood, stone, glass or metal. It can be plain or ornate; what is important is that is contains the wine used in the Rite of Wine and Cakes, or in the Great Rite.
Circle	This defines the Sacred Space of the Witch. It is created whenever and wherever it is needed. Casting the Circle is just one part of creating the Sacred Space. A Coven would traditionally cast a Circle 9 feet (2.7 m) across; however, when working on your own it should be as small or as large as your needs.
Coven	A group of three or more Witches (two would be a Partnership). Coven size varies considerably, although some consider that a 'proper' Coven should be made up of six men, six women and the High Priestess. The Coven is the family group of the Witches.
Covenor	Any member of the Coven who has taken their Coven Oath, from Aspirant to High Priestess.
Covenstead	The home of the Coven, where most of the indoor meetings and Rituals will take place. The Covenstead is usually the High Priestess's house.
Craft	One of the terms for Witchcraft, which has been rightly described as both an Art and a Craft.
Daughter Coven	The term used for a Coven which has been formed by a member of the original Coven, and is hence directly descended from the Mother Coven.

Deity	A Goddess or a God. The term 'Deities' is often used generically for all Goddesses and Gods, wherever they have come from.
Deosil	Clockwise or Sunwise. When setting up and working in your Sacred Space you should always move deosil, unless you are undoing something.
Divination	The techniques and ability to discover that which might otherwise remain hidden to us. The Tarot, Crystal Ball, Astrology, reading tea leaves, and many others are all forms of Divination. Witches tend to use the term Scrying, although strictly speaking this refers to the Dark Mirror, Cauldron, Fire or Witches' Runes.
Divine	A broader term than deity, the Divine encompasses both the Goddess and the God and includes those aspects which do not have a gender or a name.
Elements	The term Elements is often used to refer to Earth, Air, Fire and Water. However, it is important that the fifth Element, that of Spirit, which we ourselves bring to the Circle, is not forgotten. The Elements are the keystones of the Craft and also refer to aspects of ourselves as well as to energies around us.
Esbat	The Witches' term for Full Moon meetings or workings.
Fith-fath	An image, usually created from wax or clay, of a person, made so as to direct magic towards that person.
Goddess and God	The female and male aspects of the Divine. However, the term 'the Gods' is often used to denote both.
Great Rite	This is the symbolic union of the Goddess and the God. Generally it is performed with the Chalice and Athame; the exceptions to this are between working partners and in some forms of Initiation.

Handfasting	One of many Rites of Passage, Handfasting is the name for the Witches' wedding. It differs from most 'orthodox' kinds of wedding in that both parties enter as equals and make their own individual vows to each other. Handfastings can be of different pre-arranged durations.
High Priestess/High Priest	The leader of a Coven is usually the High Priestess. She may lead jointly with her High Priest, but holds ultimate authority and responsibility. Some groups are run by the High Priest alone, usually where there is no female of sufficient experience to take this role.
Hive Off	The process by which one or more Witches from the Mother Coven set up their own group, with the blessing of the High Priestess of the Mother Coven.
Initiate	An Initiate of any degree, including the High Priestess.
Initiation	Initiation literally means 'to begin'. However, in the Craft Initiation is seen as the permanent declaration an individual makes to their Gods. Many of the paths within the Craft refer to three degrees of Initiation, each denoting a different level of attainment and ability.
Lore	Knowledge handed down from generation to generation. Originally oral tradition, a lot of the old lore is now finding its way into books. Much ancient lore which was thought, in our scientific age, to be superstition is now being proven and accepted.
Magic	The ability to create change by force of will. It is worth remembering that many things we take for granted, like electricity, would have been considered magic by our ancestors.
Mother Coven	The Coven that the High Priestess came from and/or the Coven from which the new Coven descends.

Occult	Literally, the word means 'hidden'. In medicine, 'occult blood' simply means blood that has been found through testing because it cannot be seen with the naked eye. Today, Occult is often used as a semi-derogatory term for anything which is not understood and is therefore feared.
Orthodox	A term I have used to identify those beliefs which people tend to think of as older than the supposedly 'New Age' beliefs, when in fact the reverse can be said to be true. For example, people tend to think that Christianity is an older belief system than the modern Pagan beliefs, when in fact the origins of Paganism (including Witchcraft) vastly pre-date it.
Pagan	This is a generic term for a number of pre-Christian religions – Druids, Witches and Heathens to name a few. 'Pagan' probably comes from the word *paganus*, referring to those who didn't live in the towns, a version of country-bumpkin if you like! Alternatively, it could come from the word *pagus*, being an administrative unit used by the occupying government. Either way, it was originally used as an insult, now it is a 'label' worn by many with pride.
Partnership	Two Witches who work together. They are frequently, but not always, a couple who are partners in daily life too.
Pathworking	A form of guided meditation in which you take a journey, which leads to an opportunity to discover more than you already know. Sometimes also referred to as 'interactive guided meditation'.
Pentacle	This is a five-pointed star with the points touching but not overlapping a circle. It symbolizes the five Elements together with the Circle of power. The Pentacle is worn by many Witches, but is also currently very fashionable, so you cannot be sure whether the wearer is of the Craft or not.

Pentagram	This is a five-pointed star not enclosed in a circle, which also symbolizes the five elements and, like the pentacle (above), can also be worn. However, the main uses of the pentagram are in invoking and banishing. Whilst there are different invoking and banishing pentagrams for each of the elements, the most commonly used is the invoking pentagram of Earth which is drawn by starting at the top point and moving deosil and continuously around the whole five points. As the invoking Pentagram must be complete, six lines are drawn, the last being a repeat of the first.
Perennials	Plants which continue to grow for more than two years. Some go on pretty much forever.
Pot on	The process of transferring a pot plant to a larger-sized pot. Potting on should only involve going one, or perhaps two, sizes up.
Priest and/or Priestess	In the Craft we are each our own Priest or Priestess, and need no one to intercede with or interpret our Gods for us.
Quarters	The four cardinal points of the compass – north, south, east and west – which are linked to the directions of the Elements.
Reincarnation	To believe in reincarnation is to believe that we return to this world many times, as many different individuals.
Rite	A small piece of Ritual which, although complete in itself, is not generally performed on its own, such as the Rite of Wine and Cakes. A series of Rites put together are a Ritual.
Rites of Passage	These rites are specific to marking the change from one stage of life to another, such as birth, marriage and death. Their names in the Craft – Wiccaning, Handfasting and Withdrawal – are different from those in current use, which reflects the different emphasis that Witches place on these events. There are other Rites of Passage but they are less common even in the Craft today.

Ritual	A series of Rites put together to achieve a specific result.
Sabbat	A seasonal festival. There are eight Sabbats in the Witches' calendar, which together are often referred to as the Wheel of the Year. Sabbats are traditionally times of great celebration and festivity. Many of the old Sabbats are still celebrated, under more modern names, for example, Yule is known as Christmas, Samhain as Halloween, and many more.
Sacred Space	For many religions their place of worship, or religious centre, is a building. Witches create their Sacred Space wherever and whenever they need it, and their magical workings, and some of their celebrations, take place within its boundaries.
Scrying	The Witches' term for divination, especially when carried out using a Dark Mirror or the Witches' Runes.
Sigil	A symbol devised to indicate someone or something. A Sigil can contain a lot of information, for example two people's names and their Sun signs. It is better to devise your own Sigils rather than to use those made by others.
Solitary	A Witch who works on her or his own.
Soul mate	This is a term used to describe a person with whom you have continuing links which persist from one lifetime to another. It does not, as is commonly misconstrued, imply that these two people will always be lovers or romantic partners through different lifetimes. A soul mate could just as easily be found in a parent, relative or even a really close friend.
Spells and Spellcraft	A spell is a set of actions and/or words designed to bring about a specific magical intent. Spellcraft is the ability, knowledge and wisdom to know when, as well as how, to perform such actions.
Star sign	See Sun sign, below.
Strong Hand	For a person who is right handed this will be their right hand, for someone who is left handed it is their left. The strong hand is sometimes called the 'giving hand'.

Sun sign	The sign of the Zodiac under which a person is born. It is the Zodiacal house that the Sun was in at the time of birth and therefore their Sun sign. Other planets will be in other houses and can therefore be thought of as Moon sign, Mars sign, and so on.
Summerlands	The Witches' name for the place our spirit goes to between incarnations, where we rest and meet with those who have gone before us, and where we choose the lessons we will learn in our next life.
Thurible	Also sometimes called a censer, this is a fireproof container designed to hold burning charcoal and loose incense. Unlike a censer, it does not have to have either a lid or chains, as it is intended to sit on the Altar.
Training Coven	A Coven which will take on newcomers, including those with no experience of the Craft, and actively encourage them to learn, grow and develop in the Craft.
Visualization	This is seeing with the mind's eye, so strongly that it appears no different from 'reality'. Visualization is not just about seeing though; when you are skilled at it, all your senses will be involved. For example, when visualizing the Element of Air you will feel the wind touch your hair and skin, hear its passage through the trees and smell the scents of Spring. Visualization is one of the key factors in working the Craft and performing magic.
Wand	A piece of wood the length of its owner's forearm. In some traditions the wand is only used where the Athame is not; in others the wand and Athame can be interchanged.
Weed	No particular types of plant are weeds per se. A weed is simply a plant in a place where you do not want it. Don't let others discourage you from growing the plants you want because of prejudice!
Wheel of the Year	This is the term used to describe the eight Sabbats as a whole and refers to the fact that they form a complete and repeating cycle.

Wicca and Wiccan	Wicca has been largely adopted as a more 'user friendly' term for Witchcraft. Personally, I do not describe myself as a Wiccan as it simply leads to the question, 'What does that mean?' and any explanation will sooner or later end up leading to the word Witch. There are some who consider that those who call themselves Wiccans are less traditional than Witches.
Widdershins	Anticlockwise and the opposite of deosil.
Wild flowers	These are plants which grow along our hedgerows and roadsides. They are usually self-seeding and a lot are garden escapees! Many species are protected and should not be picked. If you want to grow wild flowers then either get them from a supplier or take one or two seeds from a place where the plants are prolific.

TAKE IT FROM

HERE ...

There are a great many excellent books available today on the Craft. I have not tried to list them all here but have selected some of those which I have found useful. This might be in a general way, or because they specialize in a particular area which is too complex to be covered in an all-round text. Many of these books are intended to be used as reference, rather than to be read as literature. If a book is not listed here it does not mean it is not a valuable work, nor is it intended as a slight to the author. Equally, not every book here will suit every reader, as each has his or her own requirements in terms of content, and preferences when it comes to style. If you find yourself reading something you find tedious or 'heavy going', do not feel that you have a problem, it may simply be that you and that work are not compatible. You may find some of these books are out of print, however, it should be possible with perseverance to locate them through the library system. In any case, I would always recommend trying to get hold of a book through a library, at least in the first instance. In this way you can see if you like it before deciding to own a copy.

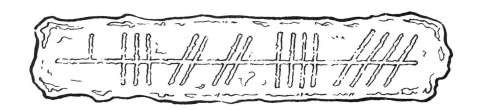

OTHER WORKS BY KATE WEST

Real Witchcraft: An Introduction, co-written with David Williams, 1996. A basic introduction to the Craft. Reprinted 2003 by I-H-O Books, Mandrake Press (formerly published by Pagan Media Ltd as *Born in Albion*).

Pagan Paths, Pagan Media Ltd, 1997. Six Pathworking cassettes covering the Elements, the Goddess and the God. These are available from the Children of Artemis, see below.

Pagan Rites of Passage, Mandrake Press, 1997. A series of booklets giving information and rituals for the Rites of Passage of Handfasting, Naming and the Rites of Withdrawal.

The Real Witches' Handbook, Thorsons, HarperCollins, 2000. Real Witchcraft for real people with real lives, this book shows how to practise the Craft in a way sensitive to those around you.

The Real Witches' Kitchen, Thorsons, HarperCollins, 2002. Oils, lotions and ointments for Magic and to relieve and heal. Soaps and bathing distillations for Circle and Magical work. Magical incenses, candles and sachets to give or to keep. Food and drink to celebrate the Sabbats, for personal wellbeing and to share with friends.

A Spell in your Pocket, Element Books, HarperCollins, 2002. A handy pocket-sized gift book for the Witch on the move.

The Real Witches' Coven, Element Books, HarperCollins, 2003. A complete guide to running a Coven. Problems and solutions, and real-life examples of what can, and does, happen. For the new, or would-be, High Priestess and/or High Priest this covers all the aspects you need to know. For the experienced High Priestess/High Priest, there are new insights and stories you will relate too. For the would-be Coven member, this tells you what to expect!

The Real Witches' Book of Spells and Rituals, Element Books, HarperCollins, 2003. Spells for all occasions, Rituals for seasonal festival, Rites of Passage and Initiations, and much more.

USEFUL BOOKS ON GARDENING AND HERBLORE

Kenneth A Beckett, David Carr & David Stevens, *The Contained Garden*, Winward, an imprint of WH Smith and Sons, 1982. It says on the cover that it is 'A complete illustrated guide to growing outdoor plants in pots', and it is! An invaluable source of ideas for creating a garden in even the smallest space, and ways of using pots to enhance the larger garden.

Scott Cunningham, *Cunningham's Encyclopaedia of Magical Herbs*, Llewellyn, 1985. Magical uses and tales surrounding most common herbs.

Mrs M Grieve, *A Modern Herbal*, Jonathan Cape, 1931; reissued Tiger, 1992. A detailed reference for the serious herbalist: identification, preparation and use of herbs, ancient and modern. Also available on the Internet at http://www.botanical.com/botanical/mgmh/mgmh.html.

Ellen Evert Hopman, *A Druid's Herbal*, Destiny Books, 1995. A Druidic view of the Wheel of the Year and the herbs which are associated with the festivals.

Roger Phillips, *Wild Flowers of Britain*, Macmillan, 1977. An encyclopaedia of the flowers of the countryside, including many 'escapees' from cultivation, with excellent identifying pictures.

Deiter Podlech, *Herbs and Healing Plants*, Collins Nature Guides, HarperCollins, 1996. A handy lightweight field guide designed for everyone interested in medicinal plants.

Doreen Valiente, *Natural Magic*, Phoenix, 1975. The magic of nature and the natural world, traditional country wise-craft.

GENERAL BOOKS ON THE CRAFT

JW Baker, *The Alex Sanders Lectures*, Magickal Childe, 1984. A perspective on Alexandrian Witchcraft.

Rae Beth, *Hedgewitch*, Phoenix, 1990. Solitary Witchcraft, written as a series of letters to newcomers.

Janice Broch and Veronica MacLer, *Seasonal Dance*, Weiser, 1993. New ideas for the Sabbats.

Janet and Stewart Farrar, *A Witches' Bible* (formerly *The Witches' Way* and *Eight Sabbats for Witches)*, Phoenix, 1996. Alexandrian Craft as it is practised.

Gerald Gardner, *The Meaning of Witchcraft*, Rider & Co, 1959; reissued by Magickal Childe, 1991. Gardnerian Witchcraft.

Pattalee Glass-Koentop, *Year of Moons, Season of Trees*, Llewellyn, 1991. Information on the tree calendar and ideas to incorporate at the Full Moons.

Paddy Slade, *Natural Magic*, Hamlyn, n.d. A perspective on Traditional Witchcraft incorporating much seasonal herbalism and plant lore.

Doreen Valiente, *ABC of Witchcraft*, Hale, 1973. Gardnerian Craft written in 'dictionary' form.

Doreen Valiente, *The Charge of the Goddess*, Hexagon Hoopix, 2000. A collection of the poetry and thoughts from the 'Mother of Modern Witchcraft'. Compiled and published after her death, this work gives a unique insight into the development of the modern Craft.

BOOKS ON PARTICULAR ASPECTS OF THE CRAFT

Anne Llewellyn Barstow, *Witchcraze*, HarperCollins, 1995. Detailed history of the persecution of Witches.

Jean Shinola Bolen, *Goddesses in Everywoman*, HarperCollins, 1985. A guide to finding the Goddess within, and a wealth of tales about the aspects of the Goddess.

Scott Cunningham, *Cunningham's Encyclopaedia of Crystal, Gem and Metal Magic*, Llewellyn, 1988. Magical properties of most gemstones available today.

Scott Cunningham, *The Complete Book of Oils, Incenses and Brews*, Llewellyn, 1989. Magical preparation and use of oils, incenses and other mixtures.

Janet and Stewart Farrar, *The Witches' Goddess*, Hale, 1987. Examination of some of the more common Goddesses.

Janet and Stewart Farrar, *The Witches' God*, Hale, 1989. Examination of some of the more common Gods.

Marian Green, *A Calendar of Festivals*, Element Books, 1991. Descriptions of festivals, not just Pagan or Wiccan, around the year with practical things to do, make and cook.

Paul Katzeff, *Moon Madness*, Citadel, 1981. A study of the effects of the Moon and many of the legends and mythologies associated with it. Not an easy read, but well worth the effort.

Kate Marks (compiler), *Circle of Song; Songs, Chants and Dances for Ritual and Celebration*, First Circle Press, 1999. As it says, songs, dances and chants from many different belief systems, many of which can be used to enhance your Rituals. Comes with a CD so you can actually hear what they should sound like!

Patricia Monaghan, *The Book of Goddesses and Heroines*, Llewellyn, 1981. A definitive guide to major and minor Goddesses from around the world.

Jeffrey B Russell, *A History of Witchcraft*, Thames & Hudson, 1983. A factual history of the Craft.

Egerton Sykes, *Who's Who Non-Classical Mythology*, Oxford University Press, 1993. A dictionary of Gods and Goddesses.

Bill Whitcomb, *The Magician's Companion*, Llewellyn, 1993. Possibly the 'ultimate' reference work for correspondences and symbols.

OTHER PUBLICATIONS WHICH MAY BE OF INTEREST

Children of Artemis, *Witchcraft and Wicca*, top quality bi-annual magazine written by Witches for Witches. Articles, poetry, Rituals, spells, art, crafts and events, and much more.

Clarissa Pinkola Estes, *Women who Run With the Wolves*, Rider, 1993. This is not a book on the Craft. However, it discusses the hidden meanings behind many tales and fables, and as such it opens the mind to the interpretation of stories which may have suffered through time and translation. Whilst this 'self-help' book is written for women it does have relevance for both genders.

Terry Pratchett, *Witches Abroad, Wyrd Sisters, Masquerade, Lords and Ladies, etc.* Corgi
Books. I recommend these books for their powers of relaxation and the
regeneration of a sense of humour after a hard day. They are pure fiction and give
a humorous perspective on the world of fictitious (?) Witches!

POINTS OF CONTACT

The following organizations facilitate contact, or provide information on Witchcraft
and Paganism. Please always enclose a stamped addressed envelope, and remember that
some of these organizations may not allow membership to people under the age of 18.

For further information on getting in touch safely with other Witches or Groups
please read the advice in *The Real Witches' Handbook*.

The Children of Artemis
Initiated Witches who seek to find reputable training Covens for genuine seekers.
Their magazine *Witchcraft and Wicca* is almost certainly the best on the Craft today
and their website is outstanding. BM Box Artemis, London WC1N 3XX. The
Children of Artemis also offer support functions and safe communication arenas for
those under the age of 18 years. http://www.witchcraft.org.
E-mail: contact@witchcraft.org

ASLaN
Information on the care and preservation of Sacred Sites all over Britain.
http://www.symbolstone.org/archaeology/aslan.
E-mail: andy.norfolk@connectfree.co.uk

The Hearth of Hecate
The website of the author's group of Covens. http://www.pyewacket.demon.co.uk

The Witches' Voice
One of the best American sources of information about the Craft. PO Box 4924,
Clearwater, Florida 33758–4924, USA. http://www.witchvox.com

Inform
Totally independent and not aligned to any religious organization or group. Their
primary aim is to help people by providing them with accurate, objective and up-to-
date information on new religious movements, alternative religions, unfamiliar belief
systems and 'cults'. Houghton Street, London WC2A 2AE. 020 7955 7654.

AJN Landscape Consultants
The Cottage, Crowan, Praze, Camborne, Cornwall TR14 9NB. Andy is an excellent
source of information on gardens, plants, nature-friendly gardening and landscaping
ideas. He has kindly said that he is willing to have his details published here and
would try to answer Pagan- and Wiccan-related gardening questions. You can contact
him on andy.norfolk@connectfree.co.uk

INDEX

Elements 2–3, 6, 13, 14, 22–3, 38–40, 97, 148, 152, 160
  invoking Ritual 43–5
  plant associations 121
  symbols 41–2
environment 10–11
Eostar 87, 120, 150
Esbat 4, 150
evening primrose 140

family life 101–2
Faunus 121
feeding 116, 135
fennel 68
fertility 30, 126
  of the land 90–1
Fire 3, 13, 14, 38, 39, 40, 41, 42, 48, 49, 97, 121, 148, 149, 152
fith-fath 160
Flora 120
fountains 106
friendship 60, 101–2, 126
Full Moon 16, 18, 20, 22, 23, 31, 46, 51, 127, 131

garden ornaments 41–2
Gardner, Gerald 153, 158
Gardnerian Witchcraft 153, 154
garlic 68–9
Goddess and God 2, 3, 6, 13, 14, 22–3, 26–7, 97, 146–7, 149, 152, 160
  garden for see contemplation area
  plant associations 120–1
  seeking blessing 16–17, 30–1, 43, 81–2
goldenrod (Solidago), 69
Great Rite 160
Green Man 42, 104, 143

Halloween 141

Handfasting 161
happiness 126
harvest Ritual 94–6
healing 4, 59, 126
  see also medicinal garden
health 59, 126
hearing 123
heartsease (wild pansy) 140
heather 140
Hecate 146
Hedgewitches 147, 153
herb paths 81
herblore 4, 152
herbs see medicinal garden; medicinal plants
Hereditary Witchcraft 153, 154
Herne 26, 146
High Priest 147, 154, 161
High Priestess 147, 154, 161
hive off 161
Holly King 2, 91–2, 101, 120
Horned God 3
horseradish 69
housing 134
Hunter 120
Hyacinthus 121
hyssop 70

Imbolg 2, 22, 84, 85–7, 122, 142, 150
indoor garden 8, 109–18
  continuing care 115–18
  planning 109–12
  pot plant Ritual 116–18
  using 112–14
Initiate 161
Initiation 161
insect repellents 75, 92
intuition 61
Iris 120
Isis 146

jimson weed see thorn apple
journals 102

Jupiter 124

knowledge 59

lavender 29, 70–1, 140
law of threefold return 149
lemon balm 70
light 11, 109–10
Litha 2, 84, 91–3, 122, 143, 150
lore 161
lovage 71
love and romance 60, 99, 126
luck 59, 126
Lugh 121, 150
Lughnasadh (Lammas), 2, 22, 84, 94–6, 122, 143, 150
lunar gardening 127–33

mad dogweed see skullcaop
Madron 2, 84, 96–8, 122, 143, 150
magic 149, 161
  plants for 59–61, 119–26
  see also spell garden
Maiden 2, 3, 86, 120, 127, 130, 146, 150
Maize Mazes 94, 143
marigold 71, 140
marjoram 71
Mars 123
maypole 90
medicinal garden 62–83
  blessing, dedicating and consecrating 81–2
  continuing care 82–3
  planning 80–1
medicinal plants 65–76
  drying and storing 78
  gathering 77–8
  magical enhancement 79–80
meditation 34
melissa see lemon balm